# Learning to Pass

# CLAiT Plus

## 2006

## Unit 2

**Ruksana Patel
& Penny Hill**

**www.heinemann.co.uk**

✓ Free online support
✓ Useful weblinks
✓ 24 hour online ordering

**01865 888058**

**Heinemann**

*Inspiring generations*

Heinemann Educational Publishers
Halley Court, Jordan Hill, Oxford OX2 8EJ
Part of Harcourt Education

Heinemann is the registered trademark of
Harcourt Education Limited

First published 2005

10 09 08 07 06 05
10 9 8 7 6 5 4 3 2 1

British Library Cataloguing in Publication Data is available
from the British Library on request.

10-digit ISBN: 0 43546343 8
13-digit ISBN: 978 0 43546343 4

Typeset by TechType, Abingdon, Oxon


Original illustrations © Harcourt Education Limited, 2005
Cover design by Wooden Ark Studio
Printed by Bath Colourbooks
Cover photo: © Getty Images

**Acknowledgements**
Every effort has been made to contact copyright holders of material reproduced in
this book. Any omissions will be rectified in subsequent printings if notice is given
to the publishers.

Microsoft product screenshots reprinted with permission from Microsoft
Corporation.

The authors would like to express their grateful thanks to Lake District Mountain
Rescue Association for permission to use their statistics. We would like to thank
Abdul Patel, Stephe and Mur Cove for working through the book and the tasks
and for providing invaluable feedback. Thank you to Brian and Rebecca Hill,
Fayaz and Fozia Roked for thier help, encouragement and support. Thank you to
Gavin Fidler and Lewis Birchon for their invaluable input which has improved the
quality of the book and for their constant support, advice and patience during the
production process. And finally, we would like to thank each other for "being there
for each other".

# Contents

An introduction to the qualification, the Quick reference guides, Practice task and Preparation for the assessment can all be found on the CD-ROM that accompanies this book.

## Who this book is suitable for

This book is suitable for:

○ candidates working towards: OCR Level 2 Certificate/Diploma for IT Users (CLAiT Plus), and OCR ITQ qualification

○ use as a self-study workbook – the user should work through the book from start to finish

○ tutor-assisted workshops or tutor-led groups

○ individuals wanting to extend their skills in Microsoft Office Excel 2003 (default settings are assumed).

Although this book is based on Excel 2003, it may also be suitable for users of Excel 2002 (XP) and Excel 2000. Note that a few of the skills may be slightly different and some screen prints will not be identical.

# UNIT 2: Manipulating spreadsheets and graphs

## Chapter 1     *Manipulating spreadsheets*

This book is written for one unit of the CLAiT Plus syllabus. Separate books are available for each of the other units. A compendium book containing units 1, 2 and 3 is also available.

In Unit 2, you need to use spreadsheet software to open existing datafiles, enter, edit and manipulate data, use formulae and common functions to calculate results, link live data from one spreadsheet to another, sort spreadsheet data and use filters to select data. You will also need to present data using graphs and charts, select and control data sources, and use formatting and alignment techniques in both spreadsheets and graphs.

You will use a software program called Microsoft Office Excel 2003 which is part of Microsoft Office 2003. Excel is a program that allows you to perform calculations, manipulate, analyse and present data. We will refer to it as Excel from now on.

This book assumes knowledge of Level 1 skills in creating and editing a spreadsheet, entering simple formulae to make calculations, creating simple graphs using Microsoft Excel 2003, and Level 1 spreadsheet terms.

## How to work through this book

This book is divided into two chapters:

**Chapter 1**
- in Section 1 you will learn to open datafiles, save files in Excel and apply formatting
- in Section 2 you will learn to identify, input and amend data
- in Section 3 you will learn to use formulae and functions
- in Section 4 you will learn to change the page setup and print spreadsheets
- in Section 5 you will learn to link spreadsheets and sort data using AutoFilter.

**Chapter 2**
- in Section 1 you will learn how to select data for charts and how to create exploded pie charts
- in Section 2 you will learn how to create comparative charts and how to define the data series

- in Section 3 you will learn how to create line-column graphs
- in Section 4 you will learn how to create xy scatter graphs.

1 Before you begin this unit, make sure that you feel confident with the basics of using Excel to create and edit a spreadsheet, enter simple formulae and create simple graphs. These skills are covered in the Level 1 book *Learning to Pass New CLAiT Unit 2*.

2 If there are some terms you do not understand, refer to the Definition of terms section on page 86.

3 Work through the chapter in sequence so that one skill is understood before moving on to the next. This ensures understanding of the topic and prevents unnecessary mistakes.

4 Read the ▶▶ *How to...* guidelines which give step-by-step instructions for each skill. Do not attempt to work through the How to... guidelines, but read the instructions and look at the screenshots. Make sure that you understand all the instructions before moving on.

5 To make sure that you have understood how to perform a skill, work through the **Check your understanding** task following that skill. You should refer to the How To... guidelines when doing the task.

6 At the end of each section is an **Assess your skills** table. Read through these lists to find out how confident you feel about the skills that you have learned.

7 **Quick reference guides** can be found on the CD-ROM that accompanies this book. You should refer to these whilst doing the Build-up tasks that follow them, the Practice task on the CD-ROM, and also during an assessment.

8 A CD-ROM accompanies this book. On it are the files that you will need to use for the tasks. Instructions for copying the files are provided below. The solutions for all the tasks can be found on the CD-ROM in a folder called **L2U2SG_worked**.

Note: there are many ways of performing the skills covered in this book. However, this book provides guidelines that have proven to be easily understood by learners.

## Files for this book

To work through the tasks in this book, you will need the files from the folder called **L2U2SG_files**, which you will find on the CD-ROM provided with this book. Copy this folder into your user area before you begin.

 *copy the folder L2U2SG_files from the CD-ROM*

1 Insert the CD-ROM into the CD-ROM drive of your computer.

2 Close any windows that may open.

3   From the desktop, double-click the **My Computer** icon to display the **My Computer** window.

4   Under **Devices with Removable Storage**, double-click on the CD-ROM drive icon to view the contents of the CD-ROM.

5   Click once on the folder **L2U2SG_files**.

6   The folder will be highlighted (usually blue).

7   In the **File and Folder Tasks** box, click **Copy this folder**.

8   A **Copy Items** dialogue box will display.

9   Click on the user area to which you want to copy the folder **L2U2SG_files**.

10  Click on **Copy**.

11  The folder **L2U2SG_files** is copied to your user area.

TIP!

It is advisable to copy and paste a second copy to another folder in your user area as backup.

## Preparing your work area

You are advised to prepare your user area in order to keep your files for Unit 2 organised. An example of a well organised folder structure is listed below:

○ create a folder for your CLAiT Plus work

○ in this folder, create a subfolder for all the CLAiT Plus units that you will be doing

○ in each unit subfolder, create further subfolders, for example:

  • **U2 working** Your working folder in which all working files will be saved

  • **L2U2SG_files** The source files folder copied from the CD-ROM

  • **L2U2SG_worked** The worked copies folder copied from the CD-ROM.

## Terms and symbols used in this book

| TERM | METHOD |
|---|---|
| **Click** | Press and release the **left** mouse button once. |
| **Double-click** | Quickly press and release the left mouse button **twice**. |
| **Drag** | Press and hold down the left mouse button while moving the mouse. |
| **Select** | Click on an item, or highlight text. |
| **Right-click** | Press the **right** mouse button once. |
| **+** | Used to indicate that two keys should be held down together, e.g. Alt + Enter – hold down the **Alt** key then press the **Enter** key. |
| **→** | Indicates that a new instruction follows. |

**In this section you will learn how to:**

○ open a .csv file

○ save a .csv file as an Excel workbook

○ select adjacent and non-adjacent cells

○ apply formatting to multiple cells

○ locate a cell containing specific data

○ wrap cell contents

○ apply vertical and horizontal alignment

○ set text orientation

○ merge cells

○ add a border

○ format numeric data to integer

○ format numeric data to 2 decimal places

○ format numeric data as currency

○ format numeric data as percentages.

## Understanding .csv files

A .csv file is a generic datafile saved in a format that can be read by most systems and in a large number of software applications. Some formatting may be lost, but the data can be read.

A spreadsheet that has been saved in a .csv format will retain any figures generated by formulae, but the underlying formulae will be lost. If any of the figures in the cells used to generate the formulae are amended the figures in the formulae column will not update to reflect the change.

Figures 2.1 and 2.2 show examples of the same spreadsheet saved as an Excel file and as a .csv file. Both files have been reopened in Excel. The spreadsheet view is the same, but the formula view shows that the underlying formula has been lost in the .csv file (Figure 2.2).

Numeric formatting (e.g. a number formatted to two decimal places) will be retained in a .csv file, but any 'hidden' figures after the decimal place will be lost. If, for example, in the original spreadsheet the figure 2.3333 had been formatted to two decimal places, when this is saved in .csv format only 2.33 would be retained. Only significant figures after the decimal

Spreadsheet view

| | A | B | C |
|---|---|---|---|
| 1 | 2 | 2 | 4 |
| 2 | 4 | 4 | 8 |
| 3 | 6 | 6 | 12 |

Formula view

| | A | B | C |
|---|---|---|---|
| 1 | 2 | 2 | =SUM(A1:B1) |
| 2 | 4 | 4 | =SUM(A2:B2) |
| 3 | 6 | 6 | =SUM(A3:B3) |

FIGURE 2.1 Data in an Excel file

Spreadsheet view

| | A | B | C |
|---|---|---|---|
| 1 | 2 | 2 | 4 |
| 2 | 4 | 4 | 8 |
| 3 | 6 | 6 | 12 |

Formula view

| | A | B | C |
|---|---|---|---|
| 1 | 2 | 2 | 4 |
| 2 | 4 | 4 | 8 |
| 3 | 6 | 6 | 12 |

FIGURE 2.2 The same data imported into Excel from a .csv file

point will be retained in a .csv file (e.g. a figure is shown as 234.00 in the spreadsheet, only 234 will be retained in the .csv file).

A .csv file is only able to save one worksheet. If multiple worksheets are contained in a workbook each worksheet must be saved individually with a different name. A graph cannot be saved in .csv format.

### ▶▶ How to... open a .csv file in Excel

1 Load Excel, either from the Start menu or by double-clicking on the desktop icon.

2 On the Standard toolbar, click on the **Open** icon.

3 The Open dialogue box will display (Figure 2.3). Locate the folder in which your file is stored.

4 Click on the drop-down arrow on the right-hand side of the **Files of type** box.

5 Click on **All Files**.

6 Select the file that you want to open by clicking on it.

7 Click **Open**.

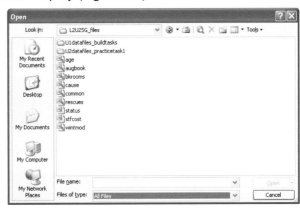

FIGURE 2.3 The Open dialogue box

### ▶▶ How to... save a .csv file as an Excel file

1 In the Menu bar, click on **File**.

2 In the drop-down menu, click on **Save As**.

3 The **Save As** dialogue box will display (Figure 2.4).

4 Click on the drop-down arrow on the right-hand side of the **Save as type** box.

5 From the list of file types, select **Microsoft Office Excel Workbook**.

TIP!

After opening a .csv file widen all columns to familiarise yourself with the data (you may also wish to print) then close the file **without** saving. Reopen the file to begin a task.

To widen all columns, click in an *empty* cell in the first row of the spreadsheet, press **Ctrl + A**, click **format** in the Menu bar, click **Column** from the drop-down menu and select **Autofit Selection**.

TIP!

Microsoft Office Excel Workbook will be at the top of the list.

TIP!

A workbook can consist of many worksheets. When you open a .csv file in Excel the program will automatically rename the worksheet with the name of the .csv file.

6 Click the drop-down arrow next to **Save in**.

7 Locate the folder in which you want to save the file.

8 In the **File name** box, enter the required filename.

9 Click on **Save**.

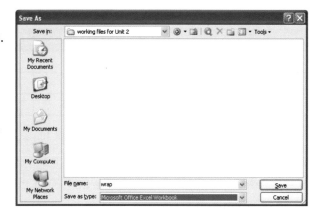

FIGURE 2.4 The Save As dialogue box

## Check your understanding *Open and save a .csv as an Excel workbook*

1 Open Excel.

2 From within Excel, open the .csv file **augbook**.

3 Widen all columns to display all data in full.

4 Study the data contained in the spreadsheet (you may wish to print).

5 Close the file without saving.

6 Reopen the .csv file **augbook**.

7 Save the file in your working area as an Excel workbook using the filename **wedaug**.

8 Close the spreadsheet file.

## Formatting text in a spreadsheet

To allow you to work more efficiently and to make the spreadsheet easier to read it will be necessary to format your spreadsheet. You will need to locate the cell(s) that contains the data you wish to format. It is generally quicker to use the Find facility in Excel (see page 16).

### Basic formatting

Use the Formatting toolbar to apply basic formatting, such as bold, italic and to change font size.

In OCR assignments you may be asked to format data to be large, medium and small.

○ Large should be the largest size.

○ Medium should be a size in-between large and small.

◎ Small should be the smallest size.

The following sizes are given as a guide:

| DESCRIPTION | FONT SIZE |
|---|---|
| Small | 10–12 |
| Medium | 14–16 |
| Large | 18+ |

## Formatting multiple cells

If you wish to apply the same formatting to multiple cells this can be done in one action by selecting all the cells then applying the formatting.

### Selecting cells

To make the application of formatting more efficient, you can select all cells that are to have the same format and then apply the formatting. The following table describes how to select the required cells.

**TIP!**

When you have selected a range of cells do not click in the spreadsheet with your mouse or you will deselect all cells.

| SELECTION | ACTION |
|---|---|
| A single cell | Click in the cell, or use the cursor (arrow) keys to move to the cell. |
| A range of adjacent cells (two or more cells that are next to each other on a sheet) | Click the first cell in the range then: <br> when the white cross appears, drag to the last cell, *or* <br> hold down **Shift** then click in the last cell in the range, *or* <br> press **F8** and use the arrow keys to highlight the cells to be selected. <br><br> (You can scroll to make the last cell visible.) |
| A range of non-adjacent cells | Click in the first cell, hold down the **Ctrl** key, click in each cell to be included. When all cells have been selected, release the **Ctrl** key. |
| All cells in the worksheet | Click in the **Select All** button, *or* <br> click in any *empty* cell in the first row of the spreadsheet then press **Ctrl+A**. <br> |
| All cells in a section (area) | Click in any cell in the section then press **Ctrl+A**. |
| Non-adjacent cells or cell ranges | Click on the first cell (or highlight the first range), then hold down **Ctrl** while you select the other cell(s) or ranges, *or* <br> select the first cell or range of cells and then press **Shift + F8** to add another non-adjacent cell or range to the selection. <br> Note: If you make a mistake when selecting non-adjacent cells you will need to cancel the selection and start again as you cannot deselect individual cells or ranges. |

 **How to...** *format multiple cells using the Format Painter*

1 Click in one of the cells to be formatted.

2 Apply the required formatting.

3 Double-click on the Format Painter icon 🖌 in the toolbar.

4 Select (highlight) all cells to apply the same formatting.

5 When all cells have been formatted click on the Format Painter icon again (or press **Esc**) to deselect it.

**TIP!**

To copy formatting to a single cell you only need to single-click the format painter.

**How to...** *locate a cell containing specific data*

1 In the Menu bar, click on **Edit.**

2 In the drop-down menu, click on **Find**.

3 The **Find and Replace** dialogue box will display.

4 In the box next to **Find what** enter the text contained in the cell that you wish to locate.

5 Click on the **Find Next** button.

6 Click on **Close** to exit the Find and Replace dialogue box. The cell containing the specified data will be selected.

**TIP!**

You do not need to match case when keying text in the **Find what** box.

**How to...** *wrap cell contents*

1 Select the cell(s) that contain the data you wish to wrap.

2 In the Menu bar, click on **Format.**

3 In the drop-down menu, click on **Cells**.

4 Click on the **Alignment** tab in the **Format Cells** dialogue box.

5 In the **Text control** section, click to insert a tick in the box next to **Wrap text** (Figure 2.5).

6 Click on **OK**.

7 The cell contents will now be wrapped.

8 If necessary, adjust the column width and/or row height to ensure words are not split and/or data is displayed on the specified number of lines.

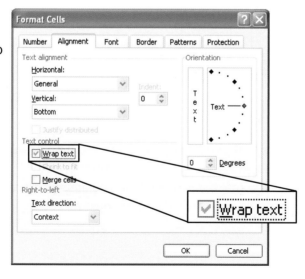

FIGURE 2.5 Wrap text in the Format Cells dialogue box

**TIP!**

If a column is wide enough to display the data on one line, text wrap will have no effect. If you cannot reduce the column width without hiding data you can force the text to wrap.

To force text to wrap, or to choose where to wrap, click in front of the text to be displayed on the next line then press **Alt + Enter**.

1   Reopen your saved file **wedaug**.

2   Format the cells containing the following data with a bold font and wrap the cell contents on to two lines:

ROOM PER NIGHT

WEDDING PLAN

COST PER HEAD

FLOWERS PER HEAD

WEDDING COST

ROOMS REQUIRED

3   Locate the cell containing **CHARGE PER ROOM** and wrap the cell contents on to three lines.

4   Adjust column widths to ensure that words in the wrapped cells are not split and that all data is displayed in full.

5   Save the file in your working area as an Excel workbook using the filename **wrap**.

6   Close the spreadsheet file.

**▶▶ How to...** *apply vertical and horizontal alignment*

1   Open the spreadsheet file in Excel.

2   Select the cell(s) to be formatted.

3   Click on **Format** in the Menu bar.

4   Click on **Cells** in the drop-down menu.

5   In the **Format Cells** dialogue box, click on the **Alignment** tab.

6   In the Text alignment section, click on the drop-down arrow in the box under **Horizontal** (Figure 2.6).

7   Select the required horizontal alignment.

8   Click on the down arrow in the box under **Vertical** (Figure 2.6).

9   Select the required vertical alignment.

10  Click **OK** (unless you want to apply other formatting).

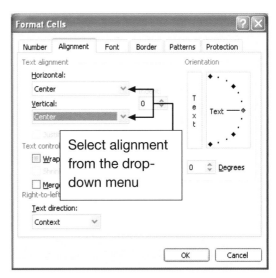

FIGURE 2.6 Setting text alignments in the Format Cells dialogue box

**How to...** *set text orientation*

1 Select the cell(s) containing the text to be orientated.

2 In the Menu bar, click on **Format**.

3 In the drop-down menu, click on **Cells**.

4 Click on the **Alignment** tab in the **Format Cells** dialogue box.

5 In the **Orientation** section, either:

   a Click and drag the text marker up or down until the required number appears in the box next to **Degrees**, or

   b Enter the required number in the box to the left of **Degrees** (or use the up/down arrows).

6 Click **OK**.

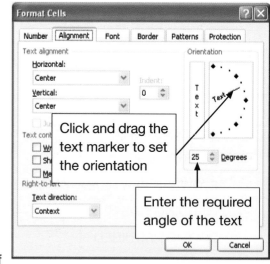

FIGURE 2.7 Setting the text orientation in the Format Cells dialogue box

**TIP!**

If text orientation is set to a minus figure (e.g. –25 degrees) the text will start at the top of the cell and flow down (this is sometimes referred to as clockwise because the hands of a clock move around the clock in this direction).

If the direction is a plus figure (e.g. 25 degrees) then the text will start at the bottom of the column and flow up (this is sometimes referred to as anti-clockwise because the text will flow in the opposite direction to the hands of a clock).

**Check your understanding** *Set horizontal and vertical alignment and text orientation*

1 Open your saved file **wrap**.

2 Format the data as listed in the table below.

| COLUMN LABELS | HORIZONTAL ALIGNMENT | VERTICAL ALIGNMENT | TEXT ORIENTATION |
|---|---|---|---|
| **WEDDING PLAN** and **COST PER HEAD** | Left | Bottom | |
| **CUSTOMER – INVOICE** (Columns A–I) | Centre | Centre | |
| **PLAN: BRONZE( A15)** **PLAN: SILVER (A21)** **PLAN: GOLD (A26)** | Centre | Centre | 25 degrees |

3 Save the file as an Excel workbook using the filename **align**.

4 Close the spreadsheet file.

**▶▶ How to...** *merge cells*

1 Open the spreadsheet in Excel.

2 Select the cells to be merged.

3 Click on **Format** in the Menu bar.

4 In the drop-down menu, click on **Cells**.

5 In the **Format Cells** dialogue box, click on the **Alignment** tab.

6 In the **Text control** section, click to insert a tick in the box next to **Merge cells** (Figure 2.8).

7 Click on **OK**.

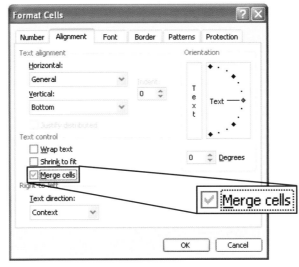

**TIP!**

Click the **Merge and Centre** icon  on the toolbar to merge cells and centre the data across the merged columns in one action.

FIGURE 2.8 Merge cells in the Format Cells dialogue box

**▶▶ How to...** *add a border*

1 Select the cells to be framed with a border.

2 On the **Standard Toolbar**, click the drop-down arrow to the right of the Borders icon ▦ .

3 Select the **Outside Borders** or **Thick Box Border** option (Figure 2.9).

**TIP!**

Select the Thick Box Border as this displays more clearly on the print.

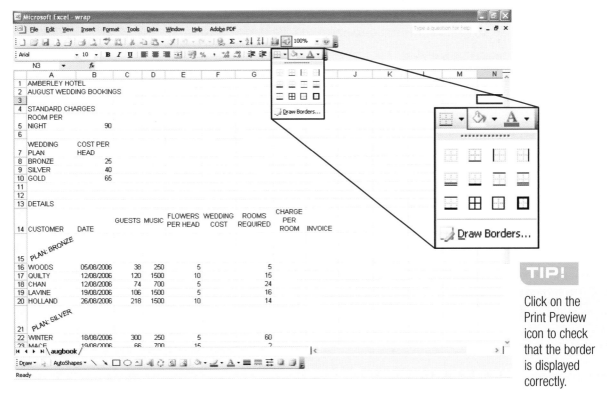

**TIP!**

Click on the Print Preview icon to check that the border is displayed correctly.

FIGURE 2.9 The drop-down borders menu

1   Open your saved file **align**.

2   Format the data listed in the table below.

| LABELS | SIZE AND STYLE | COLUMNS |
|---|---|---|
| AMBERLEY HOTEL | Large | Centred across all columns containing data: Columns A–I Framed by a border |
| AUGUST WEDDING BOOKINGS | Medium | Centred across all columns containing data: Columns A–I |
| STANDARD CHARGES | Small, bold | Centred across all columns A–B Framed by a border |
| WEDDING PLAN | Small, bold | A |
| COST PER HEAD | Small, bold | B |
| DETAILS | Small, bold | Centred across all columns containing data: Columns A–I Framed by a border |
| CUSTOMER – INVOICE | Small, bold | A–I |
| PLAN: BRONZE PLAN: SILVER PLAN: GOLD | Small, bold | A |

3   Check the formatting in **Print Preview**.

4   Save the file as an Excel workbook using the filename **merge**.

5   Close the spreadsheet file.

## Formatting numeric data in a spreadsheet

The 'default' format in Excel is 'general'. When you enter numeric data, this format will allow you to see all the figures exactly as you enter them (e.g. with the exception of zeros, all numbers after the decimal point will be visible). The results generated by formulae will also show the appropriate number of figures after the decimal point. Whilst it is useful to show the 'true' value, it does not always make the figures easy to read and you will probably want to apply a numeric format to give a more consistent display.

There are many formats for numeric data. The most common formats are integer (0 decimal places) and 2 decimal places. However, you can select to display as many decimal places as you wish. Changing the formatting of the numeric data does not change the underlying figure – just the way it looks on the spreadsheet.

In the spreadsheet that follows, the formula **A2*B2** has been entered in cell **C2**.

Note that the result generated by the formula in C2 does not change when the formatting of cell **A2** is changed.

Decimal places in an Excel worksheet:

|   | A | B | C |
|---|---|---|---|
| 1 | FIGURE 1 | FIGURE 2 | TOTAL |
| 2 | 1.4 | 10 | 14 |

Column A formatted to 1 decimal place

|   | A | B | C |
|---|---|---|---|
| 1 | FIGURE 1 | FIGURE 2 | TOTAL |
| 2 | 1 | 10 | 14 |

Column A formatted to Integer

**▶▶ How to...** *format numeric data to integer or 2 decimal places*

1 Select the cell(s) to be formatted.

2 Click on **Format** in the Menu bar.

3 In the **Format Cells** dialogue box, click on **Cells**.

4 Click on the **Number** tab.

5 In the **Category** section, select **Number**.

6 Click on the up/down arrows to the right of the **Decimal places** box to select the required number of decimal places.

7 In the box under **Negative numbers** click on the required format (Figure 2.10).

8 Click on **OK**.

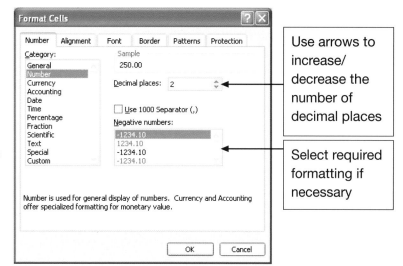

Use arrows to increase/decrease the number of decimal places

Select required formatting if necessary

FIGURE 2.10 The number formatting options

Monetary amounts can be formatted to currency. When currency format is selected you can choose to display the figures with or without the currency symbol and may also display the figures to integer or select any number of decimal place(s).

Negative numbers may be displayed in black or red with the minus sign in front of the number (e.g. –4.30). They may also be displayed in red without the minus sign. If you are printing in black and white you should avoid this option as the printed sheet may not clearly show that the numbers are negative!

Care must be taken when entering figures that will be formatted to percentage, date and time.

| FORMAT | CORRECT DATA ENTRY | RESULT OF CORRECT ENTRY WHEN FORMATTED | INCORRECT DATA ENTRY | RESULT OF INCORRECT ENTRY WHEN FORMATTED |
|---|---|---|---|---|
| Percentage | Either 4% or 0.04 | 4% | 4 | 400% |
| Date | 12/6/05 (/ separates day/ month/year) | 12/06/2005 | 12.6.05 | 12.6.05 (this is treated as text and therefore cannot be calculated) |
| Time | 10:15 (: separates hours from minutes) | 10:15 | 10.5 | 03:36:00 |

**▶▶ How to...** *format numeric data to currency*

1 Select the cell(s) to be formatted.

2 Click on **Format** in the Menu bar.

3 In the drop-down menu, click on **Cells**.

4 In the **Format Cells** dialogue box, click on the **Number** tab (Figure 2.11).

5 In the Category section, select **Currency**.

6 Click on the up/down arrows to the right of the **Decimal places** box to select the required number of decimal places.

7 In the box under **Symbol** click on the drop-down arrow then click on the required currency symbol (may be none).

8 In the box under **Negative numbers** click on the required format.

9 Click on **OK**.

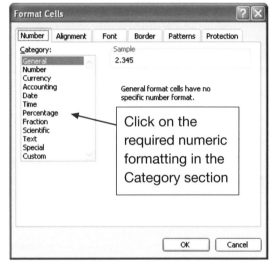

FIGURE 2.11 The Number tab in the Format Cells dialogue box

**▶▶ How to...** *format numeric data to percentage*

1 Select the cell(s) to be formatted.

2 Click on **Format** in the Menu bar.

3 In the drop-down menu, click on **Cells**.

4 In the **Format Cells** dialogue box, click on the **Number** tab.

5 In the **Category** section, select **Percentage**.

6 Click on the up/down arrows to the right of the **Decimal places** box to select the required number of decimal places.

7 Click on **OK**.

**TIP!**

When you are required to use the currency symbol you should always use the currency symbol appropriate to the country in which you are working. In the UK this will be £. In Southern Ireland it will be €.

## Check your understanding *Formatting numeric data*

1   Open your saved file **merge**.

2   In the **DETAILS** section format the figures under the column labels **GUESTS** and **ROOMS REQUIRED** to number and integer (0 decimal places).

3   Format the figures under the column labels **MUSIC** and **FLOWERS PER HEAD** to currency and integer (0 decimal places) with a currency symbol.

4   Format **all** the figures in the **STANDARD CHARGES** section to currency and 2 decimal places with a currency symbol.

5   In the **DETAILS** section check that all figures under the **DATE** column are formatted to English date format (day/month/year).

6   Save the file in your working area as an Excel workbook using the filename **numcur**.

7   Close the spreadsheet file.

## ASSESS YOUR SKILLS – Open a datafile, save as an Excel file and apply formatting

By working through Section 1 you will have learnt the skills listed below. Read each item to help you decide how confident you feel about each skill:.

- ○ open a .csv file
- ○ save a .csv file as an Excel workbook
- ○ select adjacent and non-adjacent cells
- ○ apply formatting to multiple cells
- ○ locate a cell containing specific data
- ○ wrap cell contents
- ○ apply vertical and horizontal alignment
- ○ set text orientation
- ○ merge cells
- ○ add a border
- ○ format numeric data to integer
- ○ format numeric data to 2 decimal places
- ○ format numeric data as currency
- ○ format numeric data as percentages.

If you think that you need more practice on any of the skills in the above list, go back and work through the skill(s) again.

If you feel confident, move on to Section 2.

# 2: Identify, input and amend data

## LEARNING OUTCOMES

**In this section you will learn how to:**

○ *use Find and Replace*

○ *insert text and numeric data*

○ *amend text and numeric data*

○ *insert a row/column*

○ *delete a row/column*

○ *clear the contents of a cell/row/column*

○ *move text and numeric data.*

## Inputting and amending data

When you input and amend data in a spreadsheet it is very important that you enter the data accurately. Numeric data must be entered with 100 per cent accuracy.

If you are editing an existing spreadsheet, look carefully at how the original data has been entered. Make amendments/additions in the same case as the original data and ensure that the data entered is formatted in the same way as the existing data in the spreadsheet.

### Using Find and Replace to edit data

In Section 1 you used the Find facility to locate data. On some occasions you may need to replace data that appears in several places on the spreadsheet. Although this could be done manually, it is far more efficient to use Excel's Find and Replace facility. Using the Find and Replace facility will ensure that all occurrences of the data are found and will reduce the risk of error because the data will only need to be entered once.

**▶▶ How to...** *use Find and Replace*

1  In the Menu bar click on **Edit**.

2  Click on **Find** in the drop-down menu.

3  In the **Find and Replace** dialogue box click on the **Replace** tab.

4  In the box next to **Find what** enter the text to be replaced.

> **TIP!**
>
> If you want to move between cells in Excel without using the mouse:
>
> ○ pressing the **Tab** key moves to the cell to the right
>
> ○ pressing **Enter** usually moves to the cell below
>
> ○ pressing an arrow key moves one cell in the direction of the arrow.

FIGURE 2.12 The Find and Replace dialogue box

5  In the box next to **Replace with** enter the replacement text.

6  Check to ensure that you have not made any mistakes.

7  Click on the **Replace All** button.

8  Click on **Close**.

9  All instances of the original data will have been replaced.

## Check your understanding  *Use Find and Replace*

1  Open the datafile **wintmod**.

2  Ensure that all data is displayed in full.

3  Replace all instances of the word **September** with the word **October**

4  Save the file in your working area as an Excel workbook using the filename **replaced**

5  Close the file.

### ▶▶ *How to...*  insert text and numeric data

1  Click in the cell in which you want to enter data.

2  Enter the data.

3  Move to the next cell in which you wish to enter data or move to any other cell.

4  Check to ensure that the additions are correct and that numbers are 100 per cent accurate.

5  Check that the formatting of the inserted data is correct.

### ▶▶ *How to...*  amend text and numeric data

1  Click in the cell containing the data that you wish to edit.

2  Enter the new data.

3  Move to the next cell you wish to edit or move to any other cell.

4  Check to ensure that the amendments are correct and that numbers are 100 per cent accurate.

5  Check that the formatting of the amended data is correct.

## Inserting and deleting rows and columns

When you insert or delete rows or columns in your spreadsheet, Excel will update formulas by adjusting both relative and absolute cell references to reflect their new locations.

For example, if the formula in a cell was =A3+B3+$G$10 and a new column was inserted between columns A and B, Excel would automatically adjust the formula to become =A3+C3+$H$10.

Any values added in the new column B would **not** be included. If you wanted the values in the new column to be inserted you would have to adjust the formula manually.

If the formula had been =SUM(A3:B3,$G$10) Excel would adjust the formula to become =SUM(A3:C3,$H$10).

The values in column B would automatically be included.

If you want references to adjust automatically, it's a good idea to use range references (whenever appropriate) in your formulas, rather than specifying individual cells.

Note: only formulae within the range will be updated – if you add a row/column that was not included in the original formula you wil need to adjust the formula to reflect the change.

If a formula refers to a deleted cell the message #REF! will appear in the affected cell. You will need to amend the formula to reflect the changes in your spreadsheet.

## Inserting rows and columns

You may need to add rows and columns to an existing spreadsheet. When a new row is inserted it will be placed *above* the active cell. When a new column is inserted it will be placed *to the right* of the active cell.

### ▶▶ How to... insert a row

1 Click in any cell in the row immediately *below* the position in which you want the new row to be inserted.

2 Click on **Insert** in the Menu bar.

3 In the drop-down menu, click on **Rows**.

4 The new row will be inserted.

### ▶▶ How to... insert a column

1 In your spreadsheet, click in any cell in the column *to the right* of the position that you want the new column to be inserted.

2 In the Menu bar click on **Insert**.

3 In the drop-down menu, click on **Columns**.

4 The new column will be inserted.

1   Open your saved file **replaced**.

2   Insert a new row between the rows containing the data for **Room 211 and Room 215**.

3   Under the appropriate column labels enter the following data in the new row:

| AREA | MONTH | CONTRACTOR | DAYS | SUPERVISOR |
|------|-------|------------|------|------------|
| Room 212 | October | Perkins | 7 | Verity |

4   Insert a new column to the left of the column containing the data for Area (the first column).

5   Enter the label **Completed** as a label for the new column. Make sure this label is displayed in the same row as the column label **Area**.

6   Save the file in your working area as an Excel workbook using the filename **insert**.

7   Close the file.

## Deleting rows and columns

When a row or column is deleted from the spreadsheet, the data contained in the deleted row or column is permanently removed from the spreadsheet.

If you make a mistake, you can click on the **Undo** icon 🔄 but once you have re-saved the spreadsheet all data in the deleted column will be permanently lost.

▶▶ **How to...** *delete a column*

1   Click on the letter of the column you wish to delete so that the entire column is highlighted.

2   Right-click the mouse anywhere in the highlighted column.

3   In the menu, click on **Delete**.

4   The column will be deleted.

▶▶ **How to...** *delete a row*

1   Click on the number of the row you wish to delete so that the entire row is highlighted.

2   Right-click anywhere in the highlighted row.

3   In the menu, click on **Delete**.

4   The row will be deleted.

1   Open your saved file **insert**.

2   Delete the entire column containing the data for **Contractor**.

3   Delete the entire row containing the data for **Beauty Salon**.

4   Save the file in your working area as an Excel workbook using the filename **delete**.

5   Close the file.

1   Open your saved file **delete**.

2   In the **Days** column amend the figure for Pool to be **10**.

3   In the **Area** column amend Pool to be **Swimming Pool**.

4   Save the file in your working area as an Excel workbook using the filename **edit**.

5   Close the spreadsheet file.

## Clearing rows and columns

On some occasions you may wish to clear the contents of a row or column without actually deleting that row or column. Once the contents have been cleared the row or column will still be present on the spreadsheet but it will contain no data.

You can also clear the contents of part of a row or column by selecting the cells containing the data to be cleared. The advantage of clearing the contents of cells, rather than deleting the cell contents, is that when cells are cleared any formatting is also removed. When the contents of cells are deleted the data is deleted but the formatting remains.

Clearing rows and columns will have no effect on cell references in existing formulae as the row and/or column are still present.

▶▶ **How to...** *clear the contents of a column*

1   Click on the letter of the column in which you wish to clear the contents.

2   The column will be selected.

3   Check it is the correct column.

4   Right-click anywhere in the selected column.

5   In the menu, click on **Clear Contents**.

6   All data in the column will be removed but the column will remain.

**TIP!**

To clear the cell contents of part of a column or row, select only the cells to be cleared and follow the instructions for How to... clear the contents of a column/row.

1 Click on the number of the row in which you wish to clear the contents.

2 The entire row will be selected.

3 Check it is the correct row.

4 Right-click anywhere in the selected area.

5 In the menu, click on **Clear Contents**.

6 All data in the row will be removed but the row will remain.

## Check your understanding *Clear the contents of a column or row*

1 Open the datafile **bkrooms**.

2 Ensure all data is displayed in full.

3 Clear the entire contents of the 3 rows containing the following data:

○ STANDARD

○ LUXURY

○ PREMIER

4 Clear the cell containing the label **OTHER BOOKINGS** and all the data below this label.

5 Save the file in your working area as an Excel workbook using the filename **clear**.

6 Close the file.

## Moving data

Data can be moved from one cell to another by cutting and pasting or by dragging and dropping.

**▶▶ How to...** *move data using Cut and Paste*

1 Select the data to be moved.

2 Right-click anywhere in the selected area.

3 In the menu, click on **Cut**.

4 Click on the cell that is to be the new location (if you are moving a range of cells click on the cell that is to contain the data in the first cell).

5 Right-click on the selected cell.

6 In the menu, click on **Paste**.

**TIP!**

Take great care when pasting, any existing data in the target cell(s) will be overwritten when you paste the new data.

If you make a mistake, click on the **Undo** icon .

**▶▶ How to...** *move data using drag and drop*

1  Select the cell(s) containing the data to be moved.

2  Hover the mouse over an outside edge of the selected cell(s).

3  A black cross with 4-way arrows will appear ⊹.

4  Hold on the edge of the selection and drag it to the new location.

5  Release the mouse button.

6  Press a cursor key or click in a different cell to confirm the new location.

**TIP!**

If you have difficulty using the mouse, or are not confident when dragging and dropping use the cut and paste method.

**Check your understanding** *Move data*

1  Open your saved file **edit**.

2  Move the label **Winter Refurbishment Programme** to the first column of the first row.

3  Save the file in your working area as an Excel workbook using the filename **move**.

4  Close the spreadsheet file.

## ASSESS YOUR SKILLS – Identify, input and amend data

By working through Section 2 you will have learnt the skills listed below. Read each item to help you decide how confident you feel about each skill:

○ use Find and Replace

○ insert text and numeric data

○ amend text and numeric data

○ insert a row/column

○ delete a row/column

○ clear the contents of a cell/row/column

○ move text and numeric data.

If you think that you need more practice on any of the skills in the above list, go back and work through the skill(s) again.

If you feel confident, move on to Section 3.

## LEARNING OUTCOMES

**In this section you will learn how to:**

- *enter formulae*
- *use mathematical operators in formulae*
- *use brackets appropriately*
- *use relative cell references*
- *use absolute cell references*
- *use mixed cell references*
- *replicate formulae*
- *name a cell*
- *use a named cell reference in formulae*
- *use comparison operators*
- *replicate formulae using a variety of cell references*
- *use functions in formulae*
- *use the IF function*
- *use the SUMIF function*
- *use the COUNTIF function*
- *use the COUNT and COUNTA functions*
- *use the MAX and MIN functions.*

## Entering formula

A formula is a set of instructions that tells Excel to take data (the value) from a specified location (the reference) and perform a calculation. Cell (or range) references are used in formulae to enable Excel to find the data that needs to be calculated.

### Understanding cell references

A cell reference tells Excel where to find the data to be used in a formula. The type of reference (e.g. relative, absolute, named, etc.) gives further instructions about what to do if the formula is replicated (copied) or if the cell is moved.

| CELL REFERENCE | EXAMPLE | |
|---|---|---|
| Relative | =A1+B1 | When copied to the row below, the formula will become =A2+B2. |
| | | Because the copied formula is now in row 2, Excel will now use the values in row 2 to make the calculation. |
| | | The cell reference is *relative* to the position of the formula (the cell reference is changed in relation to the position of the formula). |
| Absolute | =$A$1+$B$1 | When copied to the row below, the formula will still be =$A$1+$B$1. |
| | | If this formula is copied anywhere in the spreadsheet it will still use the values from cells A1 and B1. |
| Mixed | =$A1+$B1 | When copied to the row below, the formula will be =$A2+$B2. |
| | =A$1+B$1 | If this formula is copied anywhere in the spreadsheet the values in the A and B column will always be used, the row values used will be relative to the position of the formula. |
| | | In a mixed cell reference either the row is absolute and the column is relative or the row is relative and the column absolute. |
| Named | overheads | Any cell (or any range of cells) in a spreadsheet can be given a name. This name can then be used in formula. |
| | | If a formula containing a named cell reference is copied it will always use the value in the named cell (or range) when calculating results. |
| | | The named cell (or named range) can be moved anywhere in the spreadsheet. Excel will still use the value of the named cell (or range) in the calculation. |

## Mathematical operators

Mathematical operators are used between cell references to instruct Excel how to perform the calculation. For example, A1+B1 instructs Excel to take the value in the cell A1 and add it to the value in the cell B1.

The table opposite shows the operators that you will need to use.

| OPERATOR | ACTION |
|---|---|
| + | Add |
| – | Subtract |
| * (asterisk) | Multiply |
| / | Divide |
| % | Per cent |

## Understanding brackets

When entering a formula to perform a calculation, remember the order in which any calculation will be carried out. Calculations in **brackets** are always carried out first then **divide** and/or **multiply** then **add** and/or **subtract**.

For example:

**5+2*2** will give the answer **9** because **2*2=4** then **4+5=9**.

Whereas:

**(5+2)*2** will give the answer **14** because **5+2=7** then **7*2=14**.

When you are entering a formula you must think very carefully about how you are entering it. You must include brackets around the part(s) of the formula that you want to be calculated first. Remember that a formula in a spreadsheet must always begin with = (equal sign).

Look at the spreadsheet below.

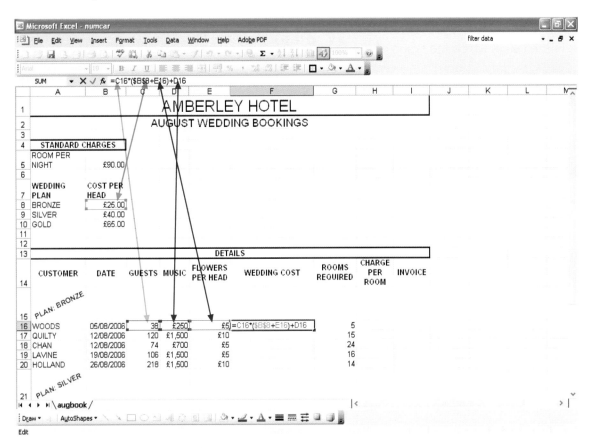

FIGURE 2.13 The cell references in a formula

The number of GUESTS has been multiplied by the (COST PER HEAD added to the FLOWERS PER HEAD) then MUSIC has been added.

The COST PER HEAD and the FLOWERS PER HEAD have been enclosed in brackets because these figures need to be added together *before* they are multiplied by the GUESTS. The figure for MUSIC has then been added.

**38*(25+5) + 250**

*Result of calculation with and without brackets*

|  | FIRST PART OF CALCULATION | SECOND PART OF CALCULATION | THIRD PART OF CALCULATION | RESULT |
|---|---|---|---|---|
| **With brackets** Add then multiply | (25+5)=30 | 30*38 =1140 | 1140+250=1390 | **Correct** |
| **Without brackets** Multiply then add | 38*25=950 | 950+5=955 | 955+250=1205 | **Incorrect** |

**▶▶ How to...** *enter a formula*

1 Click in the cell in which the result of the formula is to be displayed.

2 Enter the = sign.

3 Click in the cell (or select the range) that contains the first value (set of values).

4 Enter the mathematical operator.

5 Click in the cell (or select the range) that contains the second value (set of values).

If the formula is to be a multi-stage calculation, continue entering the mathematical operator and clicking in the cell (or selecting the range) until all stages of the calculation have been entered.

6 Check the formula, inserting brackets and absolute cell references if required.

7 Press **Enter** to complete the formula. The answer to the calculation will now appear in the cell in which you entered the formula.

**TIP!**

You can also use the keyboard to enter the required formula. If you choose to use this method, check your work very carefully to make sure you have been 100 per cent accurate.

## Using absolute, relative and mixed cell references

If a formula is to be replicated to other cells you will need to think about whether the cell references need to be relative, absolute or mixed.

Look at the spreadsheet shown in Figure 2.14. In the **WEDDING COST** column, the formula **=C16*($B$8+E16)+D16** has been entered for the first customer (WOODS).

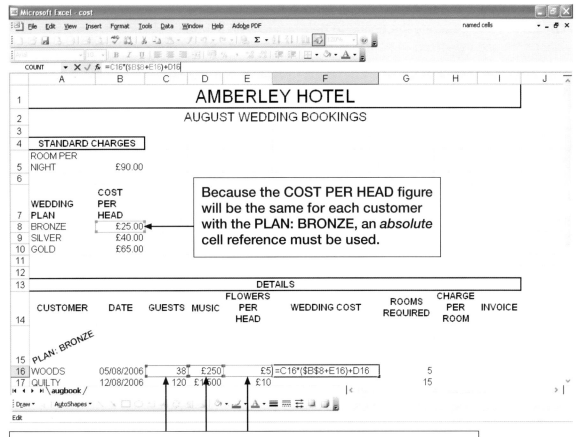

Because the COST PER HEAD figure will be the same for each customer with the PLAN: BRONZE, an *absolute* cell reference must be used.

The figures for **GUESTS**, **FLOWERS PER HEAD** and **MUSIC** are *different* for each customer, therefore *relative* cell references must be used.

FIGURE 2.14 Absolute and relative cell references in a formula

When the formula is replicated the value in the cell B8 (£25.00) will always be used in the calculation.

**▶▶ How to...** *replicate formula*

1 Click in the cell containing the formula to be replicated.

2 Position the mouse over the bottom right corner of the cell until the cursor turns into a black plus sign.

3 Hold down the mouse button and drag across the cells into which the formula is to be copied.

4 Release the mouse button.

5 The formula will be replicated into the selected cells.

**TIP!**

If there are empty rows in your spreadsheet you should not display the results of the formula (or zero values) in the blank rows. You should delete (or clear) any formula contained in blank rows.

In some calculations (such as AVERAGE and COUNT) all data (including zero values) would be included in the calculation and would result in incorrect figures! If cells are blank they are ignored.

**TIP!**

You can change between relative, absolute and mixed cell references by highlighting the cell reference you want to change then clicking on **F4** until the reference you require is displayed.

The **STAFF BONUS** and the **SECURITY** figures must be multiplied by the **NO OF GUESTS** to generate the bonus to be given to staff and the security cost from each wedding.

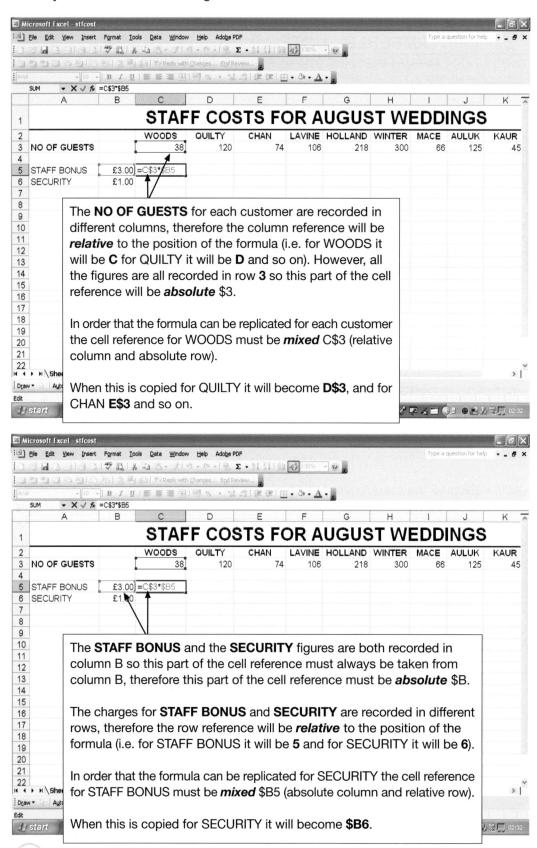

The **NO OF GUESTS** for each customer are recorded in different columns, therefore the column reference will be *relative* to the position of the formula (i.e. for WOODS it will be **C** for QUILTY it will be **D** and so on). However, all the figures are all recorded in row **3** so this part of the cell reference will be *absolute* $3.

In order that the formula can be replicated for each customer the cell reference for WOODS must be *mixed* C$3 (relative column and absolute row).

When this is copied for QUILTY it will become **D$3**, and for CHAN **E$3** and so on.

The **STAFF BONUS** and the **SECURITY** figures are both recorded in column B so this part of the cell reference must always be taken from column B, therefore this part of the cell reference must be *absolute* $B.

The charges for **STAFF BONUS** and **SECURITY** are recorded in different rows, therefore the row reference will be *relative* to the position of the formula (i.e. for STAFF BONUS it will be **5** and for SECURITY it will be **6**).

In order that the formula can be replicated for SECURITY the cell reference for STAFF BONUS must be *mixed* $B5 (absolute column and relative row).

When this is copied for SECURITY it will become **$B6**.

1   Open file **stfcost**.

2   In the **STAFF BONUS** row, in the **WOODS** column calculate the bonus generated for **WOODS** by multiplying the figure in the cell next to **STAFF BONUS** (£3.00) by the **NUMBER OF GUESTS** for **WOODS**.

You will need to use mixed cell references in this formula.

3   Replicate this formula to generate the figure for **SECURITY** for **WOODS**.

4   Replicate the formula to generate the figures for **STAFF BONUS** and **SECURITY** for all other customers (QUILTY to SMYTHE).

5   Save the file in your working area as an Excel workbook using the filename **bonus**.

1   Open your saved file **numcur**.

2   In the **DETAILS** section, in the **WEDDING COST** column, enter a formula to calculate the WEDDING COST for the first customer (WOODS):

Multiply the figure for **GUESTS** by the result of **COST PER HEAD** (BRONZE) plus **FLOWERS PER HEAD** then add the figure for **MUSIC**.

You will need to use relative and absolute cell references.

3   Replicate the formula for all **PLAN: BRONZE** customers.

4   Calculate the **WEDDING COST** for the first **PLAN: SILVER** customer (WINTER):

Multiply the figure for **GUESTS** by the result of **COST PER HEAD** (SILVER) plus **FLOWERS PER HEAD** then add the figure for **MUSIC**.

You will need to use relative and absolute cell references.

5   Calculate the **WEDDING COST** for the first **PLAN: GOLD** customer (PATEL):

Multiply the figure for **GUESTS** by the result of **COST PER HEAD** (GOLD) plus **FLOWERS PER HEAD** then add the figure for **MUSIC**.

You will need to use relative and absolute cell references.

6    Save the file in your working area as an Excel workbook using the filename **abref**.

7   Close the spreadsheet file.

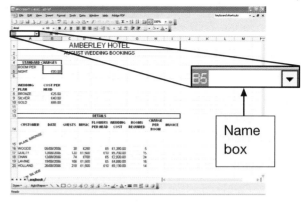

**▶▶ How to...** *name a cell*

1 Click in the cell to be named.

2 Click in the **name box** (Figure 2.16).

3 Enter the name for the cell.

4 Press **Enter**.

FIGURE 2.16 Naming a cell

---

**Check your understanding** *Name a cell*

1 Open your saved file **abref**.

2 In the **STANDARD CHARGES** section, name the cell containing the value £90.00 overnight.

3 Save the file in your working area as an Excel workbook using the filename **named**.

---

## Using a named cell in a formula

When you include a named cell in a formula, the cell name is displayed instead of the cell reference. The named cell does not have a row and column reference so it can be moved anywhere in the spreadsheet. Whenever a named cell is used in a formula Excel will locate the named cell and will use the values from the named cell in the calculation.

## Understanding functions

A function is a pre-written set of instructions that tells Excel what to do. For example, the SUM function will tell Excel to add up all the numbers in the specified cells. Some functions perform common calculations (e.g. SUM, COUNT, etc.), others allow you to create a conditional formula, for example the IF function.

An IF statement will return one value if a condition is met and another value if a condition is not met. For example, IF A1=200, return the value 'FULL' otherwise return the value 'BOOK NOW'. Excel will look at the data in cell A1. If the value is 200, the value in the cell containing the formula will be 'FULL'. If the data in cell A1 is not 200, then the value in the cell containing the formula will be 'BOOK NOW'. If you don't specify the results to be displayed if the criterion is not met, Excel will return the value

'FALSE'. To display a blank cell if the condition is not met you can press the spacebar. This will show in the formula as ' '.

Excel has numerous available functions, but you will only need to understand and use a few of these. The following table gives a brief explanation of the functions that you will need to be able to use.

| FUNCTION | WHAT IT DOES |
|---|---|
| SUM | Adds the values in a range of cells. |
| SUMIF | Adds the values of cells that meet a specified condition. |
| AVERAGE | Calculates the average of a range of cells. |
| COUNT | Counts the number of cells containing numeric data. |
| COUNTA | Counts the number of cells that contain data (numeric or alphabetic). |
| COUNTIF | Counts the number of cells that meet a specified condition. |
| MIN | Returns the smallest value from a range of cells. |
| MAX | Returns the largest value from a range of cells. |
| IF | Returns one value if a condition is met and another value if the condition is not met. |

## Comparison operators

When you use IF functions (e.g. SUMIF, COUNTIF, IF) you will need to use a comparison operator so that Excel can compare the values in the cells to see whether or not the condition is met.

| OPERATOR | ACTION |
|---|---|
| = | Equal to |
| > | Greater than |
| < | Less than |
| >= | Greater than or equal to |
| <= | Less than or equal to |
| <> | Not equal to |

**TIP!**

If the function you wish to use is not listed, enter the function, or a description of what you want to do, in the box under **Search for a function** in the Insert Function dialogue box. Excel will list the functions that best match your description.

**▶▶ How to...** *enter formulae containing a function*

1 Click in the cell in which the result of the formula is to be displayed.

2 Click on the **Insert Function** button $f_x$.

3 The **Insert Function** dialogue box appears.

4 In the **Select a Function** section, click on the required function.

5 Click on **OK**.

6 Follow the instructions below for the function you wish to enter.

FIGURE 2.17 The Insert Function dialogue box

1 Follow the instructions in How to... enter a formula.

2 In the **Function Arguments** dialogue box, click in the **Logical_test** box.

**In the Logical_test box:**

3 Click on the spreadsheet cell that contains the data that you wish to compare (e.g. F16) (or key in the cell reference).

4 Enter the comparison operator (e.g. >).

5 Enter the comparison data (a cell reference or data).

**In the Value_if_true box:**

6 Enter the result to be displayed in the cell if the condition is met (a cell reference or data).

**In the Value_if_false box:**

7 Enter the result to be displayed in the cell if the condition is NOT met (a cell reference or data).

8 Click on **OK**.

**TIP!**

To select cells to compare, click 🔣 to minimise the dialogue box. Click again to return to the full-size dialogue box.

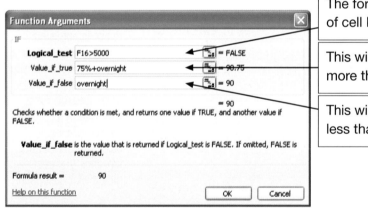

The formula looks at whether the value of cell F16 is more than 5000

This will display if the value of cell F16 is more than 5000

This will display if the value of cell F16 is less than 5000

FIGURE 2.18 The IF Function Arguments dialogue box

1 Open your saved file named **named**.

2 In the **CHARGE PER ROOM** column, use a function to calculate the figure for the first customer (WOODS):

> If the **WEDDING COST** is greater than **5000** then return 75% of the value of the named cell **room per night**, otherwise return the value of the named cell **room per night**.

3 Replicate this formula for all other customers.

4 Delete any values that are displayed in blank cells.

5 In the **INVOICE** column, use a formula to calculate the charge for the first customer:

> Multiply the **ROOMS REQUIRED** by the **CHARGE PER ROOM**, then add the figure for **WEDDING COST**.

6 Delete any values that are displayed over blank cells.

7 Format the figures in the **CHARGE PER ROOM** and the **INVOICE** columns to currency with a currency symbol and 2 decimal places.

8 Save the file in your working area as an Excel workbook using the filename **wedcomp**.

9 Close the file.

## ▶▶ How to... *use the SUMIF function*

1 Follow the instructions in How to… enter a formula.

2 In the **Function Arguments** dialogue box click in the **Range** box.

**In the Range box:**
3 Select the spreadsheet cells that contain the data to be compared (IF).

**In the Criteria box:**
4 Enter the comparison criteria (or click in a cell that contains the criteria).

In the **Range** box:
- select the spreadsheet cells that contain the data to be compared (IF).

In the **Criteria** box:
- enter the comparison criteria (or click in a cell that contains the criteria).

In the **Sum_range** box:
- select the spreadsheet cells that contain the data to be totalled if the criteria is met
- click on OK.

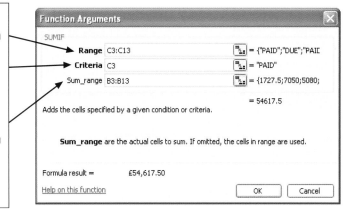

FIGURE 2.19 The SUMIF Function Arguments dialogue box

**In the Sum_range box:**

5 Select the spreadsheet cells that contain the data to be totalled if the criteria is met.

6 Click on **OK**.

1 Open the file **status**.

2 In the cell to the right of **AMOUNT RECEIVED** use a function to **TOTAL** the figures in the **AMOUNT** column **IF** the value in the **STATUS** column is **PAID**.

3 In the cell to the right of **AMOUNT DUE** use a function to **TOTAL** the figures in the **AMOUNT** column **IF** the value in the **STATUS** column is **DUE**.

4 Save the file in your working area as an Excel workbook using the filename **sumif**.

5 Close the file.

**▶▶ How to...** *use the COUNTIF function*

1 Follow the instructions in How to... enter a formula.

2 In the **Function Arguments** dialogue box, click in the **Range** box.

**In the Range box:**

3 Select the spreadsheet cells that contain the data to be compared (IF).

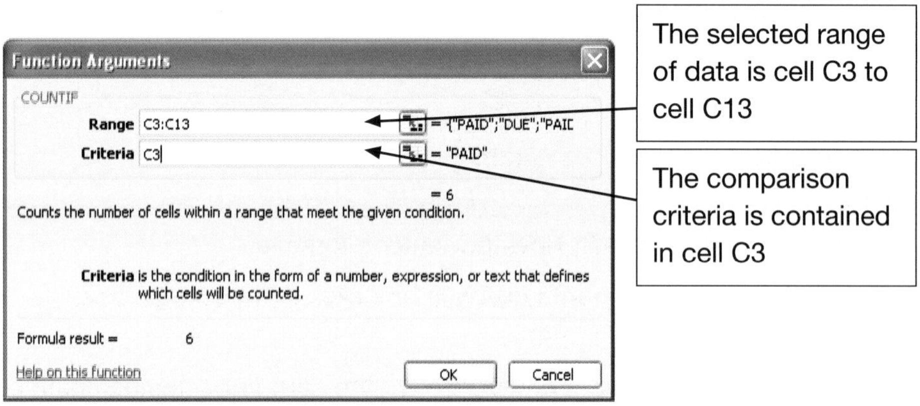

The selected range of data is cell C3 to cell C13

The comparison criteria is contained in cell C3

FIGURE 2.20 The COUNTIF Function Arguments dialogue box

**In the Criteria box:**

4 Enter the comparison criteria (or click in a cell that contains the criteria).

5 Click on **OK**.

**▶▶ How to...** *use the COUNT and COUNTA function*

The **COUNT** and the **COUNTA** functions both operate in the same way, the difference is that **COUNT** will only count numeric data and **COUNTA** will count cells that contain any data (numeric or text).

1 Follow the instructions in How to... enter a formula.

2 In the **Function Arguments** dialogue box, click in the **Value1** box.

**In the Value1 box:**

3 Select the spreadsheet cells that contain the data to be counted. (Note: empty/blank cells will not be included in the count.)

**In the Value2 box:**

4 You may add another range of cells to be included in the count or it may be left blank.

5 Click on **OK**.

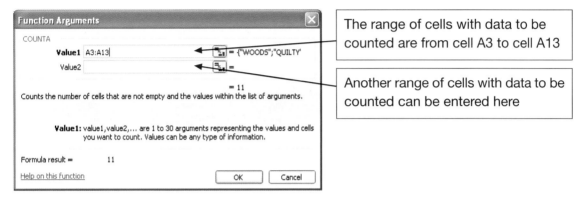

The range of cells with data to be counted are from cell A3 to cell A13

Another range of cells with data to be counted can be entered here

FIGURE 2.21 The COUNTA Function Arguments dialogue box

**Check your understanding** *Using the COUNT, COUNTA and COUNTIF function*

1 Open the file named **sumif**.

2 In the cell to the right of **NUMBER OF CUSTOMERS** use a function to count the number of **CUSTOMERS** (row 3 to row 13).

3 In the cell to the right of **NUMBER PAID** use a function to count if the value in the **STATUS** column is **PAID**.

4 In the cell to the right of **NUMBER DUE** use a function to count if the value in the **STATUS** column is **DUE**.

5 Save the file with the filename **count**

**▶▶ How to...** *use the MAX and MIN function*

The **MIN** and **MAX** functions operate in the same way.

1 Follow the instructions in How to… enter a formula.

2 In the **Function Arguments** dialogue box, click in the **Number1** box.

**In the NUMBER1 box:**

3 Select the spreadsheet cells that contain the data from which you want to return the MIN or MAX.

**In the NUMBER2 box:**

4 You may add another range of cells or it may be left blank.

5 Click on **OK**.

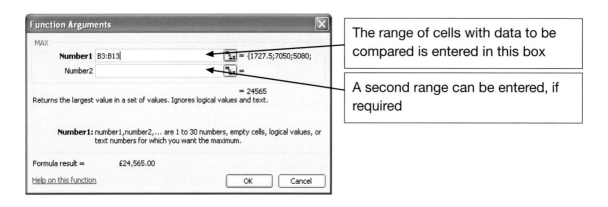

**Function Arguments**

MAX

Number1 B3:B13 ▦ = {1727.5;7050;5080;

Number2 ▦ =

= 24565

Returns the largest value in a set of values. Ignores logical values and text.

**Number1:** number1,number2,... are 1 to 30 numbers, empty cells, logical values, or text numbers for which you want the maximum.

Formula result = £24,565.00

Help on this function [ OK ] [ Cancel ]

The range of cells with data to be compared is entered in this box

A second range can be entered, if required

FIGURE 2.22 The Max Function Arguments dialogue box

## Check your understanding *Using the MAX function*

1 Open the file **count**.

2 In the cell to the right of **MAXIMUM ORDER VALUE** use a function to return the figure for the **MAXIMUM** from the AMOUNT column for the CUSTOMERS (row 3 to row 13).

3 Save the file in your working area as an Excel workbook using the filename **max**

4 Save and close any open spreadsheet files.

# ASSESS YOUR SKILLS – Use formulae and functions

By working through Section 3 you will have learnt the skills listed below. Read each item to help you decide how confident you feel about each skill:

- ⚪ enter formulae
- ⚪ use mathematical operators in formulae
- ⚪ use brackets appropriately
- ⚪ use relative cell references
- ⚪ use absolute cell references
- ⚪ use mixed cell references
- ⚪ replicate formulae
- ⚪ name a cell
- ⚪ use a named cell reference in a formula
- ⚪ use comparison operators
- ⚪ replicate formulae using a variety of cell references
- ⚪ use functions in formulae
- ⚪ use the IF function
- ⚪ use the SUMIF function
- ⚪ use the COUNTIF function
- ⚪ use the COUNT and COUNTA functions
- ⚪ use the MAX and MIN functions.

If you think that you need more practice on any of the skills in the above list, go back and work through the skill(s) again.

If you feel confident, move on to Section 4.

## LEARNING OUTCOMES

**In this section you will learn how to:**

- change the page setup
- set the page orientation
- fit to one page
- adjust margins
- insert headers and footers
- use automatic fields in headers and footers
- display gridlines and row and column headings
- print a document selection
- set and clear a print area
- hide rows and/or columns
- display formulae
- print formulae.

## Changing the page setup

A spreadsheet is easier to read if related information is printed on the same page. Although this is not always possible, amending the page setup can often improve the display.

Excel has an option to fit the spreadsheet to a specified number of pages. This is a useful option, but it can result in the size of the text being very small. Care should be taken to ensure that the spreadsheet is still readable if this option is used.

Always check the layout of the spreadsheet in Print Preview to see what, if any, adjustments need to be made.

Automatic fields can be inserted into headers and/or footers. This ensures that the date and filename will always be displayed on the document when printed.

The How to… guidelines that follow will use the Print Preview method of accessing the Page Setup window so that you can view the changes you have made.

**▶▶ How to...** *change the page orientation and fit to one page*

1  On the Standard Toolbar, click on the **Print Preview** icon .

**TIP!**

You can access the **Page Setup** window either by clicking on Page Setup within the drop-down **File** menu, or by clicking on the **Print Preview** icon and clicking on the **Setup** button.

Using the **Print Preview** method allows you to view the changes you have made before printing.

2  From Print Preview click on the **Setup** button.

3  In the **Page Setup** dialogue box, click on the **Page** tab.

4  In the **Paper size** section check that the paper size is set to **A4**, if not click on the drop-down arrow to the right of the box and select A4 from the list.

5  In the **Orientation** section, click in the radio button next to the required orientation.

6  If required, in the **Scaling** section click in the radio button next to **Fit to**.

7  Use the up and down arrows to the right of the **Fit to** boxes to specify the number of pages to fit to.

8  Make any other changes, then click on **OK**.

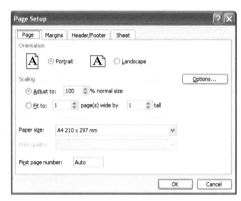

FIGURE 2.23 The Page Setup dialogue box

▶▶ **How to...** *adjust margins*

1  On the Standard toolbar, click on the **Print Preview** icon.

2  From Print Preview click on the **Setup** button.

3  In the **Page Setup** dialogue box, click on the **Margins** tab.

4  In the boxes under Top, Left, Right, and Bottom click on the up or down arrows to adjust the margins.

5  Make any other changes, then click on **OK**.

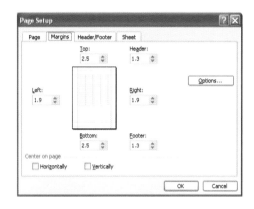

FIGURE 2.24 The Margins tab in the Page Setup dialogue box

▶▶ **How to...** *insert headers and footers and use automatic fields*

1  On the Standard toolbar, click on the **Print Preview** icon.

2  From Print Preview click on the **Setup** button.

3  In the Page Setup dialogue box, click on the **Header/Footer** tab.

4  Click on the **Custom Header** or **Custom Footer** button.

5  In the Header/Footer dialogue box, click in a section (Left, Center or Right).

6  Enter any text (e.g. your name and centre number).

7  Click in another section.

8  Click on the icon(s) for the automatic fields to be displayed.

9  Click on **OK**.

10 The **Page Setup** dialogue box will be displayed.

11 Make any other changes then click **OK**.

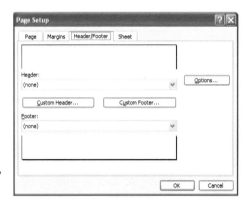

FIGURE 2.25 The Header/Footer tab in the Page Setup dialogue box

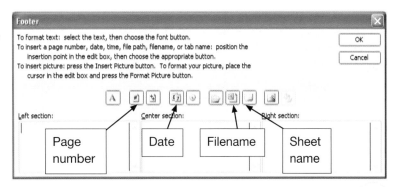

FIGURE 2.26 The Footer dialogue box

*display gridlines and row and column headings*

1  In the Standard toolbar, click on the **Print Preview** icon.

2  From Print Preview click on the **Setup** button.

3  In the **Page Setup** dialogue box, click on the **Sheet** tab (Figure 2.27).

4  Click in the box next to **Gridlines**.

5  Click in the box next to **Row and column headings** to display a tick.

6  To remove, click in the box again to remove the tick.

7  Click on **OK**.

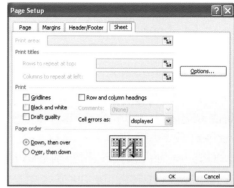

**FIGURE 2.27** The Sheet tab in the Page Setup dialogue box

**TIP!**

**Row and column headings** are the column letters, A, B, C, etc. and the row numbers 1, 2, 3, etc. Do not confuse row and column headings with the row and column labels (titles) that you enter in the cells of the spreadsheet. Displaying row and column headings is normally required on a formula printout.

## Check your understanding *Set the page layout*

1  Open your saved file **wedcomp**.

2  Set the page orientation to **landscape**.

3  Adjust the margins and/or page settings to ensure that the spreadsheet will be displayed **on one page**.

**TIP!**

Look at the spreadsheet display (in Print Preview) before entering headers and footers – try to enter headers and footers in a position that will not interfere with the spreadsheet (e.g. if you have an empty area to the right or bottom of the spreadsheet use this area).

4  Enter the following as a header or footer:

   ○ **your name and centre number**
   ○ **an automatic file name**
   ○ **an automatic date**
   ○ **automatic page numbers**.

5  Display gridlines.

6  View the spreadsheet in Print Preview.

7  Check that all data is displayed in full and will be clearly legible when printed.

8  Print the spreadsheet **wedcomp** showing the figures, on one page.

9  Save the file, in your working area, as an Excel workbook with the filename **setup**

10  Close the spreadsheet file.

# Printing a document selection

You can print part of a spreadsheet either by hiding the rows and/or columns that you do not want to print, or by selecting the data and then printing the selection. Printing a document selection is a temporary print setting – when the file is saved the print selection is lost.

In some circumstances you may only ever wish to print a particular section of the spreadsheet. In these circumstances you can set a print area. When you save the file the print area is also saved. When the document is reopened and printed only the cells in the print selection will print. If you wanted to print areas of the spreadsheet not in the print selection, the print area would need to be cleared.

Printing a document selection by selecting the cells to print will only print adjacent rows/columns on one page. For example, if you wished to print three non-adjacent columns each column would be printed on a separate page. If you wish to print non-adjacent rows/columns on one page you must hide the rows/columns that are not to be printed. When the spreadsheet is saved the rows/columns remain hidden. To print the hidden rows and columns you would need to unhide them.

**▶▶ How to...** *print a document selection*

1  Select the cells to be printed.

2  In the Menu bar, click on **File**.

3  In the drop-down menu, click on **Print**.

4  Click in the box next to **Selection** (Figure 2.28).

5  Only the selected cells will print.

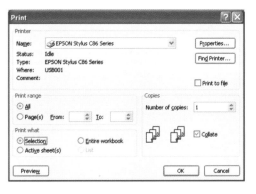

FIGURE 2.28 The Selection box in the Print dialogue box

**Check your understanding** *Print a document selection*

1  Open your saved file **setup**.

2  Select only the **DETAILS** section of the spreadsheet (columns A to I, rows 13 to 28 inclusive).

3  Print only the **DETAILS** section of the spreadsheet.

4  Close the file.

**▶▶ How to...** *set a print area*

1 Select the cells to be included in the print area.

2 In the Menu bar, click on **File**.

3 In the drop-down menu, click on **Print Area**.

4 Click on **Set Print Area**.

Whenever the spreadsheet is printed only the selected area will print.

Remember: non-adjacent cells will be printed on separate pages.

**▶▶ How to...** *clear the selected print area*

1 In the Menu bar, click on **File**.

2 In the drop-down menu, click on **Print Area**.

3 Click on **Clear Print Area**.

## Check your understanding *Set and clear a print area*

1 Open your saved file **setup**.

2 Set a print area to print only the **STANDARD CHARGES** section of the spreadsheet (columns A and B, rows 4 to 10 inclusive).

3 Print the spreadsheet showing the figures on one page.

4 Save the file in your working area as an Excel workbook with the filename **charges**

5 Clear the print area.

6 Print the entire spreadsheet showing the figures on one page.

7 Save the file in your working area as an Excel workbook with the filename **full**

**▶▶ How to...** *hide rows and/or columns*

1 Select the entire column(s) or row(s) to be hidden.

2 Position the mouse over the selected area.

3 Right-click anywhere in the selected area.

4 In the menu, click on **Hide**.

5 The column(s) or row(s) will be hidden.

**▶▶ How to...** *unhide rows and/or columns*

1 Select the entire spreadsheet. This can be done by either clicking the **Select All** button or pressing **Ctrl + A**.

2  Right-click the mouse over the row number or column letter divider where the rows or columns have been hidden.

3  Select **Unhide** from the menu.

4  The column(s) or row(s) will be revealed.

## Displaying formulae

When you display formulae, Excel will automatically widen all the columns. However, the formulae will not necessarily be displayed in full.

You can autofit the columns (select the entire spreadsheet, click **Format** in the Menu bar, select **Column** followed by **Autofit Selection**). However, this option unhides any hidden columns so they will need to be hidden again.

**▶▶ How to...** *display formulae*

1  In the Menu bar, click on **Tools**.

2  Select **Options** from the drop-down menu.

3  In the **Options** dialogue box, click on the **View** tab.

4  In the Window options section click to insert a tick in the box next to **Formulas**.

5  To return to spreadsheet view, remove the tick.

### *Printing formulae*

Formulae can be printed by following the steps in How to... print a document selection on page 41. When making a formula print in formula view you must ensure that all formulae are displayed in full – check first in Print Preview, but also check your print carefully to ensure that the formulae has been printed as you expected.

In formula view some of the formatting will not be displayed, e.g. numeric formatting (dates in the spreadsheet will display as numbers). Also, wrapped cells may not wrap. This is normal and will not affect the display in spreadsheet view.

**TIP!**

**What does it mean?**

**Spreadsheet view:** the standard presentation of a spreadsheet, all formulas are hidden and results of formulas are presented as data.

**TIP!**

To switch from the spreadsheet view to formula view and vice versa, press the **Ctrl +`** key (the accent is key usually above the Tab key or next to the spacebar).

**Check your understanding** *Print formulae*

1  Open your saved file **setup**.

2  Display the formulae.

3  Hide the entire **STANDARD CHARGES** section and the two rows that follow (rows 4 to 12).

4  Display row and column headings.

5  Ensure that all data and all formulae will be displayed in full and will be clearly legible when printed.

6  Save the file with the filename **wedform**

7  Print the formula **wedform** showing the formulae in full, on one page.

8  In your working area, save the file keeping the name **wedform**

9  Close the file.

1. Open your saved file **max**.

2. Enter your name and centre number, an automatic filename and an automatic date as footer.

3. Display gridlines.

4. Print a copy of the entire spreadsheet on one page.

5. Ensure all data is fully visible on your printout.

6. Save your file using the filename **max1**

7. Display the formulae.

8. Display gridlines and row and column headings.

9. Ensure that all formulae will be fully displayed and clearly legible when printed.

10. Save the file with the filename **maxform**

11. Save and close any open spreadsheet files.

1. Open your saved file **bonus**.

2. Set the page orientation as landscape.

3. Display gridlines.

4. Display row and column headings.

5. Enter your name and centre number as a header.

6. Enter an automatic filename and an automatic date as a footer.

7. Ensure that all data is shown in full.

8. Save the file in your working area as an Excel workbook using the filename **bonus1**

9. Print a copy of the spreadsheet showing all the figures in landscape orientation.

10. Display the formulae.

11. Print one copy of the spreadsheet showing all formulae in full.

12. Save the file in your working area as an Excel workbook using the filename **bonform**

13. Save and close any open spreadsheet files.

# ASSESS YOUR SKILLS – Identify, input and amend data

By working through Section 4 you will have learnt the skills listed below. Read each item to help you decide how confident you feel about each skill.

- ○ change the page setup
- ○ set the page orientation
- ○ fit to one page
- ○ adjust margins
- ○ insert headers and footers
- ○ use automatic fields in headers and footers
- ○ display gridlines and row and column headings
- ○ print a document selection
- ○ set and clear a print area
- ○ hide rows and/or columns
- ○ display formulae
- ○ print formulae.

If you think that you need more practice on any of the skills in the above list, go back and work through the skill(s) again.

If you feel confident, move on to Section 5.

# 5: Link spreadsheets, sort data and use AutoFilter

## LEARNING OUTCOMES

**In this section you will learn how to:**

- ○ *create a reference to a cell in another spreadsheet*
- ○ *replicate a formula containing a reference to a cell in another spreadsheet*
- ○ *use tools to sort data*
- ○ *use tools to filter data (AutoFilter).*

# Linking spreadsheets

Spreadsheets can be linked so that the values from one spreadsheet are recorded or used in the linked spreadsheet. The advantage of linking a spreadsheet, rather than copying the values into a second spreadsheet, is that a linked spreadsheet will update when changes are made to the original spreadsheet. If the data is simply copied to a new spreadsheet the values will not update.

Links can be made either to separate workbooks (a different file) or to a different sheet within the same workbook (the same file). You may use either method to link your spreadsheets.

One of the advantages of linking worksheets within the same workbook is that all related spreadsheets are kept together in one file. If the file is moved then all the related worksheets will remain together. As a result, when formulae are displayed, the reference to the linked spreadsheet will be short because it will only need to show the reference to the worksheet within the file. When separate workbooks are used, if only the file containing the linked data is open, Excel needs to show the exact location of the linked file from which it is getting the data.

Below is an example of how the formula showing the linked cell reference might look:

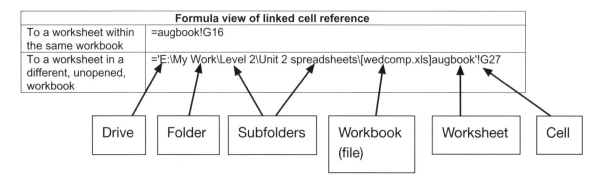

| Formula view of linked cell reference | |
|---|---|
| To a worksheet within the same workbook | =augbook!G16 |
| To a worksheet in a different, unopened, workbook | ='E:\My Work\Level 2\Unit 2 spreadsheets\[wedcomp.xls]augbook'!G27 |

Drive | Folder | Subfolders | Workbook (file) | Worksheet | Cell

You can avoid having a long linked cell reference by opening the source file before opening the file containing the link.

A link can be made to a single cell, or to a range of cells. Formulae can be entered that will enable calculations from one spreadsheet to be recorded in the other spreadsheet.

If you want to replicate the link so that the values in the adjacent cells of the original spreadsheet are also recorded in the linked spreadsheet you **must** make sure that the cell reference is **relative** (e.g. G27) before you replicate. If the link is **absolute** (e.g. $G$7) the value of the original cell in the source spreadsheet will be recorded in all cells of the linked spreadsheet. Always check the cell references before replicating.

**TIP!**

You can use **F4** to change the cell reference. Select the cell that contains the formula, in the formula bar highlight the cell reference that you want to change, press **F4**. Every time you press **F4** Excel will move through each of the possible cell references (i.e. A1, $A$1, A$1, $A1).

1  Open the source spreadsheet (the spreadsheet that contains the data that you are going to link to).

2  Open the spreadsheet that will contain the link.

3  Click in the cell in which you want the value from the source spreadsheet to be recorded.

4  Enter =.

5  Click on the source spreadsheet in the taskbar.

6  Click in the cell (or select the range of cells) that contains the data you wish to link the active cell to.

7  Press **Enter**.

8  You will be returned to the linked spreadsheet.

9  The value of the link will be recorded.

## Check your understanding *Create a reference to a cell in another spreadsheet*

1  Open your saved file **setup**.

2  Open your saved file **clear**.

3  In the **clear** spreadsheet in the **ROOMS BOOKED** column, create a link for the first HOST (cell C7) to the cell containing the figure for the **ROOMS REQUIRED** for **WOODS** (cell G16) in the setup spreadsheet. You will need to use a relative cell reference.

4  Replicate this formula for the other HOSTS.

5  In the **clear** spreadsheet in the **ROOM CHARGE** column, create a link for the first HOST (cell D7) to the cell containing the figure for the **CHARGE PER ROOM** for **WOODS** (cell H16) in the setup spreadsheet. You will need to use a relative cell reference.

6  Replicate this formula for the other HOSTS.

7  Clear any zero values (0) displayed in blank cells.

8  Format the figures in the **ROOM CHARGE** column to 2 decimal places. Do not display a currency symbol.

9  In the **clear** spreadsheet in the **NO OF ROOMS** column in the cell next to 05/08/2006 use a function to calculate the bookings for 05/08/2006 (i.e. cell B23).

   If the value in the **WED DAY** column (absolute cell reference) is 05/08/2006 (**A23** relative cell reference), total the values in the **ROOMS BOOKED** column (absolute cell reference).

10  Replicate this formula for the other dates:

   12/08/2006 (**A24**), 18/08/2006 (**A25**), 19/08/2006 (**A26**) and 26/08/2006 (**A27**).

11  Save the file in your working area using the filename **link**

12  Close any open spreadsheet files.

# Use tools to sort and filter data

## Sorting a spreadsheet

The data in the spreadsheet can be sorted in ascending or descending order by any of the columns in the spreadsheet. Be very careful to ensure that all the data relating to the sorted data also moves when the data is sorted. This is referred to as 'maintaining the integrity of data'.

**▶▶ How to...** *sort data*

1  Click in the column label containing the data to be sorted. Do **not** select the entire column unless you want to sort only the data in the selected column and not the related data.

2  In the Menu bar, click on **Data**.

3  In the drop-down menu, click on **Sort** to display the **Sort** dialogue box (Figure 2.29).

4  Check that the correct column label is shown in the **Sort by** section of the dialogue box.

5  Click in the relevant button to select the order (Ascending or Descending).

6  In the **My data range has** section check that the correct selection has been made (Header row or No header row).

7  Click **OK**.

8  The data will be sorted.

FIGURE 2.29 The Sort dialogue box

### Check your understanding *Sort data*

1  Open your saved file **move**.

2  Sort the data in ascending order of **Supervisor**.

3  Insert your name, centre number and an automatic filename as a header or footer.

4  Display gridlines and row and column headings.

5  Set the page orientation to **Portrait**.

6  Save the file using the filename **super**.

7  Print the spreadsheet showing values on one page.

8  Close the spreadsheet.

## Filtering data using AutoFilter

Using AutoFilter allows you to find records that meet specified criteria (conditions). Filtering *temporarily* hides rows. The filtered data will show only those rows that meet the criteria. Unlike sorting it will not re-arrange the data. Once the filter has been turned off, all the data in the spreadsheet will be revealed.

**▶▶ How to...** *filter data using AutoFilter*

1   Click in the column label containing the data (or highlight the column) to be filtered.

2   In the Menu bar, click on **Data**.

3   In the drop-down menu, click on **Filter**.

4   Click on **AutoFilter**.

5   Arrow buttons will appear to the right of the column label cell (Figure 2.30).

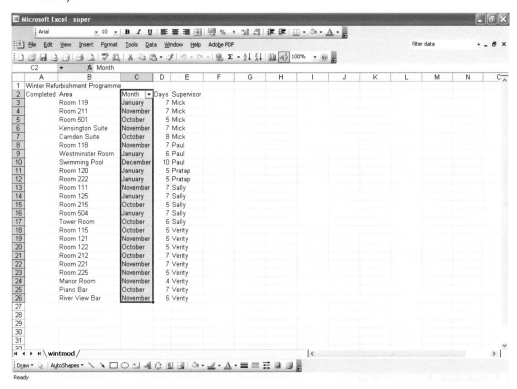

FIGURE 2.30 A drop-down button in a column to be filtered

6   Click on the drop-down arrow of the column to be filtered.

7   If the filter criterion is listed, click on it to filter the data, otherwise move on to step 8.

8   Click on **Custom** to display the **Custom AutoFilter** dialogue box (Figure 2.31).

9   Click on the drop-down arrow to the right of the **Show rows where** box.

FIGURE 2.31 The Custom AutoFilter dialogue box

10 Select the required criterion (e.g. **is greater than**).

11 In the box on the top right-hand side click on the drop-down arrow and select the comparison to be made (e.g. 5).

12 Click on **OK**.

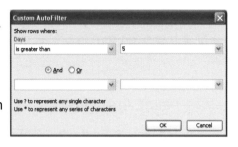

FIGURE 2.32 The criteria in the Custom AutoFilter dialogue box

**▶▶ How to...** *turn off the filter*

1 In the Menu bar, click on **Data**.

2 In the drop-down menu, click on **Filter**.

3 Click on AutoFilter.

## Check your understanding *Sort data*

1 Open your saved file **super**.

2 Filter the data to find all refurbishments where the **month** is **November**.

3 Check that your name, centre number and an automatic filename will be displayed as a header or footer.

4 Check that gridlines and row and column headings will be displayed.

5 Save the file using the filename **nov**

6 Print the filtered spreadsheet showing all the filtered data in full.

7 Turn off the AutoFilter.

8 Filter the data to find all refurbishments where the **day** is **greater than 5**.

9 Check that your name, centre number and an automatic filename will be displayed as a header or footer.

10 Check that gridlines and row and column headings will be displayed.

11 Save the file using the filename **5day**

12 Close the spreadsheet.

1   Open your saved files **setup** and **link**.

2   Using the file **link** in the column **WEDDING PARTIES** use a function to:

Count the number of weddings where the **WED DATE** is the value of the first **DATE** in the **BLOCK BOOKINGS** section (cell **A23**). You will need to use the COUNTIF function and absolute and relative cell references.

> If you are printing the formulae of a file containing links, open the source file (the spreadsheet that you linked to) first. This will prevent the linked formulae from being too long.

3   Replicate the formula for the other dates.

4   Enter your name, centre number, an automatic date and an automatic filename.

5   Display gridlines and row and column headings.

6   Save the spreadsheet using the filename **finish**

7   Print a copy of the spreadsheet showing values. Ensure all data is displayed in full.

8   Display the formulae.

9   Set the page orientation to **landscape**.

10  Check that row and column headings, your name and centre number will be displayed when printed.

11  Ensure that all formulae will be displayed on one page and will be legible when printed.

12  Print the formulae on one page.

13  Save the file with the filename **finform**

14  Close any open files and exit the software.

## ASSESS YOUR SKILLS – Link spreadsheets, sort data and use AutoFilters

By working through Section 5 you will have learnt the skills listed below. Read each item to help you decide how confident you feel about each skill.

- ○ create a reference to a cell in another spreadsheet
- ○ replicate a formula containing a reference to a cell in another spreadsheet
- ○ use tools to sort data
- ○ use tools to filter data (AutoFilter).

If you think that you need more practice on any of the skills in the above list, go back and work through the skill(s) again.

If you feel confident, move on to Chapter 2.

# UNIT 2: Manipulating Spreadsheets and Graphs

For the second part of Unit 2, you need to know how to create various types of graphs: exploded pie charts, comparative charts (bar/line), line-column graphs and xy scatter graphs.

## 1: Create exploded pie charts

### LEARNING OUTCOMES

**In this section you will learn how to:**

- understand the types and purpose of graphs
- view a datafile and identify data for a chart
- select contiguous and non-contiguous data for a pie chart
- identify the parts of a pie chart
- create an exploded pie chart
- set the chart orientation
- format numeric data on a pie chart
- emphasise one sector of a chart
- understand legends and the importance of distinctive data
- use fill effects for pie chart sectors
- set the chart to print in black and white.

## What are graphs?

Graphs (also referred to as charts) are an effective way of presenting numeric data in a visual (graphical) form. Graphs can be used to identify particular trends or patterns, sales of products, differences in performances, etc. Sometimes it can be difficult to identify important information from a spreadsheet – a visual picture of the numbers makes it easier to identify trends or changes in data.

Excel offers a wide range of graph styles and options to present data for different types of information. The chart types that you will need to create for this unit are:

| **Exploded pie charts** | Data is displayed as slices of a round pie. Each piece of the pie shows the proportion of each slice as a part of the total. |
|---|---|
| **Comparative graphs** | Used to show comparisons between categories. |

| | **Bar graphs** | Data is displayed as vertical or horizontal bars. |
|---|---|---|
| | **Line graphs** | Data is displayed as lines to show trends in data. |

| **Line-column graphs** | Data is displayed as a line with one or two columns. These show a comparison of related data against a benchmark (displayed as the line). |
|---|---|
| **xy scatter graphs** | An xy (scatter) chart either shows the relationships among the numeric values in several data series, or plots two groups of numbers as one series of xy coordinates. This chart shows uneven intervals or clusters of data. |
| **Live data modelling** | When the data in a spreadsheet is changed, the graph automatically updates, this is referred to as live data modelling. |

## Viewing a provided datafile

Before you create any chart, you should look at the data in the datafile. Check to see:

- if the data is presented in columns or rows
- if the data to be plotted on the x-axis is numeric
- which cells you will need to select for the chart. At level 2 you will be expected to select non-contiguous data.

**What does it mean?**

**Non-contiguous data** – non-adjacent data, or cells that are not next to each other.

*Understanding the selection of data for creating a chart (pie chart, bar and line graphs, line-column graphs and xy scatter graphs)*

The datafile on page 54 (Figure 2.32) lists various categories of common injuries over a period of years.

To create a pie chart to show the common injuries for the 6 subtotals for the year 2003, you would need to select the cells shown i.e. non-contiguous data.

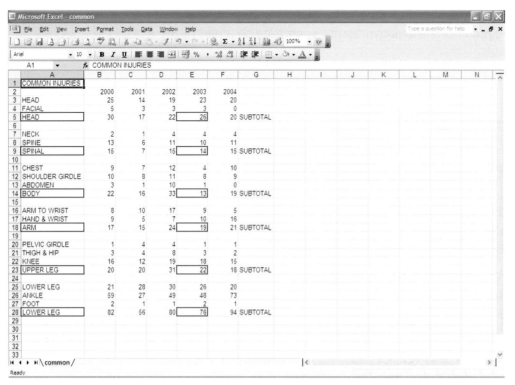

FIGURE 2.32 Non-contiguous data in a datafile (worksheet) selected to create a chart

> **▶▶ How to...** *select non-contiguous data (cells that are not next to each other)*

1  Click in the first cell containing data that you wish to use.

2  Press the **Ctrl** key down, keep it held down and click in all the remaining cells to be selected. After you have selected all the cells release the **Ctrl** key.

3  Once you have selected the data, do **not** click in any part of the datasheet, if you do, you will deselect the data.

> **▶▶ How to...** *select contiguous data (cells that are next to each other)*

### Method 1

1  Click in the first cell to be selected and drag the mouse across the range (block) of cells to the last cell to be selected.

2  A block of cells will be highlighted.

### Method 2

1  Click with the mouse in the first cell to be selected.

2  Hold the **Shift** key down.

3  Click in the last cell to be selected.

4  A range (block) of cells will be highlighted.

> Reminder: In Chapter 1 of this unit, you learnt how to:
>
> - open a csv file, display data in full and save it as an Excel file
>
> - insert headers and footers including automatic fields.
>
> Refer to pages 5 and 39 if you need to recap on these skills.

## Check your understanding Select non-contiguous data for the creation of a chart

1. Start Excel and open the file named **common**.

2. Save the file as an Excel file using the filename **injuries**

3. Display all the data in full.

4. In your file called **injuries** select the data to display the location of injuries for the **six different subtotals** (HEAD, SPINAL, BODY, ARM, UPPER LEG, LOWER LEG) for **2003**. Do not include the text SUBTOTAL.

   Check your selection of data, you should have selected the following cells:

   **A5, E5, A9, E9, A14, E14, A18, E18, A23, E23, A28, E28**

# Chart Wizard

Using the Chart Wizard makes creating graphs simple because it guides you step-by-step and presents a preview of the chart at each step. Once the chart has been created, changes can still be made to any part of it.

## The Chart Wizard steps

Step 1 Select the chart type and sub-type.

Step 2 Check the selection of cells, preview the chart and define the data series, if required.

Step 3 Select and enter, or display, the chart options e.g. Titles, Legends, Data labels.

Step 4 Select the chart location and name the chart tab (optional).

# Pie charts

A pie chart shows data as slices of a pie. The size of each slice represents the value (number) from the data on which the chart is based. A slice shows each item of data in proportion to the whole set of data. Pie charts always show only one data series and are useful to emphasise a significant element. Each slice is called a **sector**.

In Excel there are many different pie chart sub-types. You are advised to avoid selecting 3-D charts, as these can sometimes be difficult to read.

## Understanding an exploded pie chart

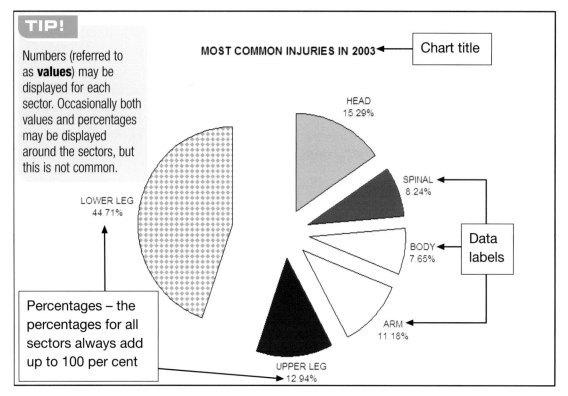

**TIP!**

Numbers (referred to as **values**) may be displayed for each sector. Occasionally both values and percentages may be displayed around the sectors, but this is not common.

MOST COMMON INJURIES IN 2003 ← Chart title

HEAD
15.29%

SPINAL ←
8.24%

BODY ←
7.65%        Data labels

ARM ←
11.18%

UPPER LEG
12.94%

LOWER LEG
44.71%

Percentages – the percentages for all sectors always add up to 100 per cent

**FIGURE 2.33** An exploded pie chart

**▶▶ How to...** *create an exploded pie chart*

1   In the datafile, select only the range of cells that contain data to be used in the pie chart.

2   Click the **Chart Wizard** 📊 icon.

3   The Chart Wizard **Step 1 of 4** dialogue box will open (Figure 2.34).

4   In the **Standard Types** tab, in the Chart type section, click on **Pie**.

5   In the Chart sub-type section, click on **Exploded Pie**.

6   Click **Next**.

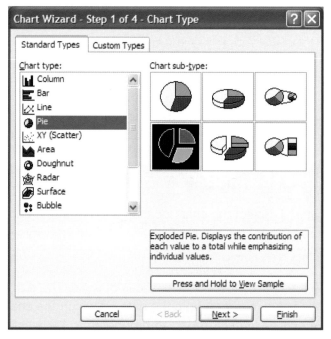

**FIGURE 2.34** The Chart Wizard Step 1 of 4 dialogue box

**7** The Chart Wizard **Step 2 of 4** dialogue box will open (Figure 2.35).

**8** A preview of the chart displays.

**9** The data range displays the selected range with the sheet name and a $ sign before the column letter and row number.

**10** Check that the preview is correct. If the preview of the chart is incorrect, click **Cancel** and start again.

**11** If the preview is correct click **Next**.

**12** The Chart Wizard **Step 3 of 4** dialogue box will open (Figure 2.36).

You will need to set options in each of the 3 tabs.

**13** Click the **Titles** tab.

**14** In the **Chart Title** box, enter the title.

**15** Click the **Legend** tab.

**16** Click to remove or place a tick in the **Show legend** box (as required).

**17** Click the **Data Labels** tab.

**18** Click to place a tick in **Category name** (if data labels are required).

**19** Click in **Value** or **Percentage** (as required).

**20** Click **Next**.

**21** The Chart Wizard **Step 4 of 4** dialogue box will open (Figure 2.37).

**22** Click in the button for **As new sheet**.

**23** Optional: enter a name for the sheet.

**24** Click the **Finish** button.

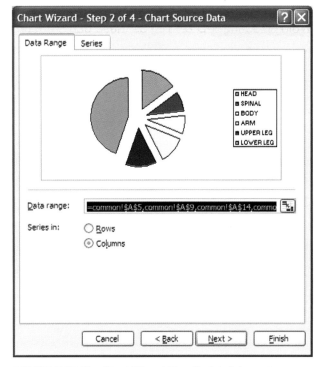

FIGURE 2.35 The Chart Wizard Step 2 of 4 dialogue box

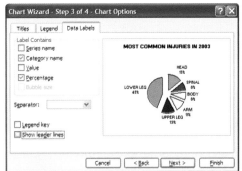

FIGURE 2.36 The Chart Wizard Step 3 of 4 dialogue box

FIGURE 2.37 The Chart Wizard Step 4 of 4 dialogue box

**TIP!**

Notice how the chart preview updates as you make changes.

**TIP!**

Click to remove the tick for Show leader lines (optional).

**TIP!**

If you are creating more than one chart in the same file, it is helpful to enter a name for the sheet. Click in the box next to **As new sheet**, delete the existing text and enter an appropriate name (Figure 2.37).

**TIP!**

If you have mistakenly created the chart on the worksheet, you can move it to a separate sheet. Right-click within the chart, a menu displays, select **Location**. A **Chart Location** dialogue box displays, click the button for **As new sheet**, click **OK**.

**▶▶ How to...** *set the chart orientation*

1  In the Menu bar, click on **File**.

2  Click on **Page Setup**. The **Page Setup** dialogue box displays.

3  In the **Page** tab, click the button for **Portrait** or **Landscape**.

4  Click **OK**.

## Check your understanding *Create an exploded pie chart*

1  In your saved file **injuries**, check that the cells you selected earlier are still selected (Check your understanding: select non-contiguous data for the creation of a chart, page 54).

2  Create an exploded pie chart to display the location of injuries using the six subtotals for 2003 that you selected.

3  Title the chart: **MOST COMMON INJURIES IN 2003**

4  Ensure that **data labels** and **percentages** are displayed for each sector.

5  Do not display a legend.

6  Create the chart on a sheet that is separate from the data source.

7  Set the chart orientation to **landscape**.

8  Save the file keeping the filename **injuries**

**▶▶ How to...** *format numeric data on a pie chart*

1  In your pie chart, click once on any of the numbers or percentages.

2  Black, square handles display around the numbers/percentages for all the sectors.

3  Right-click on any number.

4  A menu displays.

5  Select **Format Data Labels**.

6  A **Format Data Labels** dialogue box displays (Figure 2.38).

7  Click the **Number** tab.

8  In the Category section, click on the required category e.g. Number, Percentage, etc.

9  In the **Decimal Places** section, enter the required number of decimal places or use the up/down arrows.

10  Click **OK**.

FIGURE 2.38 The Number tab in the Format Data Labels dialogue box

In your pie chart titled MOST COMMON INJURIES IN 2003.

1 Format the percentages to **2 decimal places**.

2 Save the updated file keeping the filename **injuries**

## ▶▶ *How to...* emphasise a sector

1 Click once on a sector, all the sectors will be selected (black, square handles are displayed around all the sectors).

2 Click again to select only the required sector (black, square handles will display on the selected sector only).

3 Click and drag the sector outwards so that it is further away from the rest of the chart.

In your pie chart titled MOST COMMON INJURIES IN 2003.

1 Emphasise the pie chart sector with the largest percentage of injuries by pulling it further away from the rest of the chart.

2 Insert your **name** and **centre number** as a header or footer.

3 Save the updated file keeping the filename **injuries**.

## Understanding legends

A **legend** acts as a key for the data on a chart. It is a box that identifies the colours or patterns for each item of data. Legends are mainly used on comparative charts. A legend should only be displayed on a pie chart if the data labels are not displayed next to each sector. Legends should be distinctive in order to ensure that the chart is interpreted correctly.

### What is distinctive data?

If a chart displays a legend, it is very important that the legend identifies the data clearly. On the screen all the sectors are different colours, so by referring to the different colour squares in the legend, the label of each sector can be identified.

If the chart is printed in colour, the legend will still identify each sector clearly. However, if it is printed in black and white, then the sector shades will be grey and the corresponding shades in the legend will be shades of grey. This can often mean that not all of the grey shades are clearly

> **TIP!**
>
> For comparative charts, to create a legend automatically, select the row/column labels.

different on the printout, therefore it is not possible to identify the label for each sector by referring to the legend. Such a chart is unusable as it does not identify the data clearly.

There are 2 ways to make the data distinctive:

- to fill each of the sectors on a pie chart or bars on a bar chart with a different fill effect (e.g. a pattern or texture)
- to set the chart option to print in pure black and white.

**▶▶ How to...** *fill pie chart sectors with patterns*

1 Click once on a sector (all the sectors are selected), click again to select one sector (square handles will display on the selected sector only).

2 Right-click on the selected sector. A menu displays.

3 Click on **Format Data Point** in the menu.

4 A **Format Data Point** dialogue box displays.

5 Click the **Fill Effects** button.

6 A **Fill Effects** dialogue box opens.

7 Click the **Pattern** tab and select a pattern from the options.

8 To change the colour, click the drop-down arrow for **foreground** and choose a colour from the list.

9 Click **OK**. Click **OK** to close the **Format Data Point** dialogue box.

**▶▶ How to...** *set the option to print in black and white*

1 From the chart view, click the **Print Preview** icon.

2 From Print Preview click the **Setup** button Setup... .

3 A **Page Setup** dialogue box will open.

4 Click the **Chart** tab (Figure 2.39).

5 Click the button for **Print in black and white**.

6 Click **OK**.

7 The sectors will be filled with different fill effects.

8 Click **Close** to close the Print Preview.

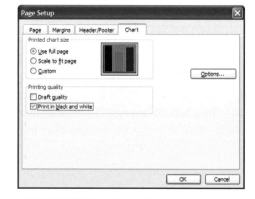

FIGURE 2.39 The Chart tab in the Page Setup dialogue box

**TIP!**

In the chart view, the different fill effects will not display, but they will usually show on the printout. Remember to check that each shade is clearly distinctive on the printout. If not, you will need to fill any indistinctive sectors/bars with a pattern.

In your pie chart titled MOST COMMON INJURIES IN 2003.

1   Set the option to print the chart in black and white.

2   Do not save the chart.

3   Print one copy of the chart.

In your pie chart titled MOST COMMON INJURIES IN 2003.

1   Fill the largest sector (LOWER LEG) with a pattern.

2   Save the updated file keeping the filename **injuries**

3   Print one copy of the chart.

4   Compare this printout with the previous printout of the pie chart.

## ASSESS YOUR SKILLS – Create exploded pie charts

By working through Section 1 you will have learnt the skills listed below. Read each item to help you decide how confident you feel about each skill.

- ○ understand the types and purpose of graphs
- ○ view a datafile and identify data for a chart
- ○ select contiguous and non-contiguous data for a pie chart
- ○ identify the parts of a pie chart
- ○ create an exploded pie chart
- ○ set the chart orientation
- ○ format numeric data on a pie chart
- ○ emphasise one sector of a chart
- ○ understand legends and the importance of distinctive data
- ○ use fill effects for pie chart sectors
- ○ set the chart to print in black and white.

If you think that you need more practice on any of the skills in the above list, go back and work through the skill(s) again.

If you feel confident, move on to Section 2.

## Bar charts

A bar chart is used to show data changes over a period of time, comparisons between individual items, or comparisons between data. A comparative bar chart displays comparisons for two or more sets of data. Data can be displayed as vertical or horizontal bars. Excel refers to a horizontal bar chart as a bar chart and a vertical (upright) bar chart as a column chart. In the UK, bar charts are usually vertical (upright bars) – therefore the column chart option in Excel should always be selected.

In Excel, there are many different bar chart sub-types. You are advised to use 2-dimensional vertical bar charts (choose the option for column chart).

## Line graphs

Line graphs are used to show trends in data at intervals, they display a set of related values plotted as a line. A marker is usually displayed for each value (data point). Comparative line graphs show trends for more than one data series.

## Understanding comparative charts

Comparative charts are a simple and effective way to show a direct comparison between data in visual form.

**x-axis labels**   are the category labels, they describe what the bars or lines represent.

**y-axis** is the value axis, it shows the numeric value (quantity).

**Legend** is a key to interpreting the data on the chart. The small boxes in the legend are used to identify each set of bars or lines.

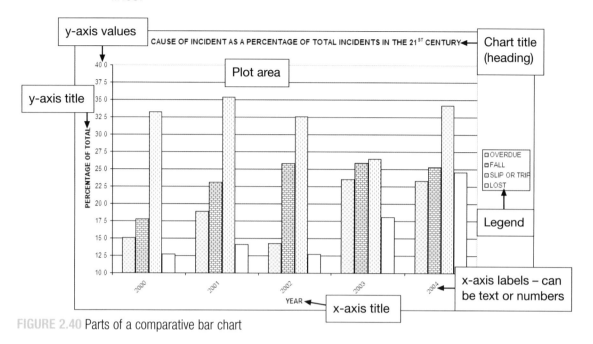

FIGURE 2.40 Parts of a comparative bar chart

## Selecting data for comparative charts

Comparative bar charts are created in exactly the same way as simple bar charts, except that more than one data series is selected. When selecting the data for a comparative chart, you should also select the cells that need to be displayed as the axis titles and the legend. Refer to How to… select contiguous data and How to… select non-contiguous data on page 54.

## Legends in comparative charts

Any comparative chart **must** display a legend. This must identify the data clearly on a printout. The small boxes in the legend are used to identify each set of bars by colour or pattern.

**▶▶ How to...** *create a comparative bar chart*

1 In the datafile, select only the relevant range of cells.

2 Click the **Chart Wizard** 📊 icon.

3 The Chart Wizard **Step 1 of 4** dialogue box will open (Figure 2.41).

4 In the **Standard Types** tab, in the **Chart type** section, click on **Column** (do not click on **Bar**).

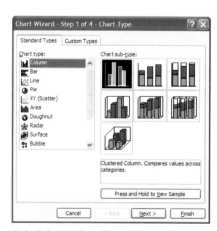

FIGURE 2.41 The Chart Wizard Step 1 of 4 dialogue box

5  In the Chart sub-type section, check that **Clustered Column** is selected.

6  Click **Next**.

7  The Chart Wizard **Step 2 of 4** dialogue box will open.

8  Check that the preview of the chart in this box is correct. If the preview is incorrect, you *must* define the data series before continuing. Refer to How to… define the data series on pages 65–67.

9  If the preview is correct, click **Next**.

10 The Chart Wizard **Step 3 of 4** dialogue box will open.

11 Click the **Titles** tab.

12 In the **Chart Title** box, enter the title.

13 In the **Category (X) axis** box, enter the x-axis title.

14 In the **Value (Y) axis** box, enter the y-axis title.

15 Click the **Legend** tab.

16 Check that there is a tick in the **Show legend** box.

17 Click **Next**.

18 The Chart Wizard **Step 4 of 4** dialogue box will open.

19 Click the button for **As new sheet**.

20 Optional: enter a name for the sheet.

21 Click **Finish**.

▶▶ **How to...** *create a comparative line graph*

1  In the datafile, select only the relevant range of cells.

2  Click the **Chart Wizard** 📊 icon.

3  The Chart Wizard **Step 1 of 4** dialogue box will open (Figure 2.42).

4  In the **Standard Types** tab, in the **Chart type** section, click on **Line**.

5  In the Chart sub-type section, check that **Line with markers...** is selected.

6  Click **Next**.

7  Follow steps 7 to 21 as described in How to… create a comparative bar chart.

FIGURE 2.42 The Chart Wizard Step 1 of 4 dialogue box

1 Open the file called **cause**.

2 Save the file as an Excel file using the filename **incidents**

3 View the data in the datafile. Note that using AutoFit to display all data in full is not appropriate for all datafiles (such as this one). Widen the columns so that all data is visible.

4 Select the data for the most common causes of rescue incidents for the five years from **2000 to 2004 inclusive**. The most common causes were **OVERDUE, FALL, SLIP OR TRIP** and **LOST**.

Check your selection of data: you should have selected the cells shown below (Figure 2.43).

| | A | B | C | D | E | F | G | H | I | J | K |
|---|---|---|---|---|---|---|---|---|---|---|---|
| 1 | CAUSE OF INCIDENT AS A PERCENTAGE OF TOTAL INCIDENTS | | | | | | | | | | |
| 2 | | 1995 | 1996 | 1997 | 1998 | 1999 | 2000 | 2001 | 2002 | 2003 | 2004 |
| 3 | OVERDUE | 13.32 | 13.23 | 14.79 | 16.26 | 15.21 | 15.11 | 18.87 | 14.29 | 23.56 | 23.28 |
| 4 | COLLAPSE | 9.05 | 5.85 | 6.85 | 10.43 | 8.09 | 4.53 | 6.13 | 4.35 | 7.18 | 8.9 |
| 5 | IN DIFFICULTY | 4.27 | 4.58 | 3.84 | 1.84 | 4.21 | 6.34 | 4.72 | 5.9 | 6.32 | 10.34 |
| 6 | FALL | 19.6 | 24.94 | 24.38 | 21.78 | 24.27 | 17.82 | 23.11 | 25.78 | 25.86 | 25.29 |
| 7 | SLIP OR TRIP | 27.89 | 28.5 | 34.25 | 30.98 | 31.72 | 33.23 | 35.38 | 32.61 | 26.44 | 34.19 |
| 8 | SHOUTS OR LIGHTS | 2.76 | 3.31 | 8.22 | 5.21 | 4.86 | 1.51 | 4.25 | 2.17 | 2.01 | 3.44 |
| 9 | LOST | 6.78 | 7.12 | 10.41 | 9.51 | 11.97 | 12.69 | 14.15 | 12.73 | 18.1 | 24.57 |
| 10 | | | | | | | | | | | |

FIGURE 2.43 Selected data in the **incidents** datafile

5 Create a **comparative vertical bar chart**.

6 Title the chart: **CAUSE OF INCIDENT AS A PERCENTAGE OF TOTAL INCIDENTS IN THE 21ST CENTURY**

7 Title the x-axis: **YEAR**

8 Title the y-axis: **PERCENTAGE OF TOTAL**

9 Ensure that the legend clearly displays the following causes:

**OVERDUE        FALL        SLIP OR TRIP        LOST**

10 Create the chart on a sheet that is separate from the data source.

11 Set the chart orientation to **landscape**.

12 Insert your **name**, **centre number**, an **automatic date** and an **automatic filename** as a header or footer.

13 Save the chart.

## Defining data series

You may need to define the data series for comparative bar and line graphs, line-column graphs and xy scatter graphs.

When creating a chart using the Chart Wizard, you must check the preview of the chart in the Chart Wizard Step 2 of 4 (Figure 2.44). You may need to define each data series so that Excel knows which row/column of data is to be used for the x-axis, the y-axis and which data should be displayed as a legend. You may also need to remove unwanted data series at this stage.

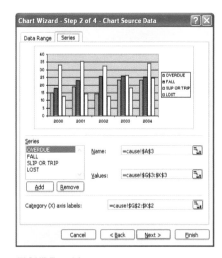

FIGURE 2.44 Defining the data series

**remove an unwanted series**

1 In the Chart Wizard **Step 2 of 4** dialogue box, click the **Series** tab.

2 In the **Series** section below the chart preview, click on the name of the unwanted series.

3 Click the **Remove** button.

4 The chart preview will change – the incorrect data set will be removed from the preview.

**select the correct data to be plotted on the x-axis**

1 In the Chart Wizard **Step 2 of 4** dialogue box, click the **Series** tab.

2 Click on the **Collapse Dialog** button next to the **Category (X) axis labels**.

3 You will see the worksheet and a small (collapsed) window (Figure 2.45).

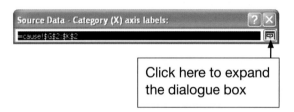

Source Data - Category (X) axis labels:

=cause!$G$2:$K$2

Click here to expand the dialogue box

FIGURE 2.45 The collapsed Chart Source Data dialogue box

4 In the worksheet, select only the cells that should display as the x-axis labels. Do not include the row/column label.

5 A marquee (dotted line) will display around the selected cells.

6 The range of cells will display in the **Category (X) axis labels box**.

7 In the collapsed window, click the **Expand Dialog** button.

8 You will return to the **Source Data** dialogue box.

**select the correct data to be plotted on the y-axis**

1 In the Chart Wizard step 2 of 4 dialogue box, click the **Series** tab.

2 In the **Series** section below the chart preview, click on the name of the incorrect series so that it is selected (highlighted).

3 Click the **Collapse Dialog** button next to **Values**.

4 In the worksheet, select the correct range of cells to be plotted on the y-axis for that series (do not include the row/column label).

5 A marquee (dotted line) will display around the selected cells.

6 The range of cells will display in the **Values** box.

7  In the collapsed window, click the **Expand Dialog** button.

8  You will return to the **Source Data** dialogue box.

**▶▶ How to...** *select the data for the remaining data series to be plotted on the y-axis*

1  In the Chart Wizard **Step 2 of 4** dialogue box, click the **Series** tab.

2  Click on the name on the second data series.

3  Repeat steps 2 to 8 in How to… select the correct data to be plotted on the y-axis.

**▶▶ How to...** *select the name for a legend item*

1  In the Chart Wizard **Step 2 of 4** dialogue box, click the **Series** tab.

2  In the **Series** section below the chart preview, click on the name displayed (e.g. this may be displayed as Series1).

3  In the **Name** section, delete any existing text. Click on the **Collapse Dialog** button. You will see the worksheet and a small (collapsed) window.

4  In the worksheet (datafile) click in the cell to be used as the name of the legend item.

5  Click the **Expand Dialog** button.

6  Repeat this process for the remaining items to be displayed in the legend.

When you have selected all the data series and checked the name of the items to be displayed in the legend:

○  check that the chart preview is correct in the Source Data window

○  click **Next**

○  continue setting the options in the Chart Wizard steps 3 and 4.

**▶▶ How to...** *format the axis values (scale, intervals, numbers)*

1  In your chart, hover the mouse pointer over any of the y-axis values (numbers).

2  A **Value Axis** Tool tip displays. If numeric data is plotted on both the x- and the y-axis, then the Tool tip will display as **Value (X) Axis** or **Value (Y) Axis**.

3  Double-click on the axis value. A **Format Axis** dialogue box opens.

**TIP!**

Changes to the axis are made once the chart is created.

**What does it mean?**

Axis scale: the scale is the minimum (lowest) value and the maximum (largest) value displayed on the x- or y-axis.

Interval: the 'gap' between the numbers (values) on the x- or y-axis. Excel refers to the interval as **major unit**.

Negative number: a number below zero, usually preceded with a minus sign.

4   In the dialogue box, click the **Scale** tab.

5   Click in the **Minimum** box, delete the existing number and enter the required minimum value. To display a negative number, type a minus sign before the number e.g. −75.

6   Click in the **Maximum** box, delete the existing number and enter the required maximum value.

7   Click in the **Major unit** box, delete the existing number and enter the required interval.

When you enter minimum, maximum values and intervals (major unit), the tick in the box is removed. This ensures that the values remain set. If the values you are required to set are already displayed, you must click in the check box to remove the tick otherwise Excel may change the minimum or maximum value (Figure 2.46).

8   Click the **Number** tab (Figure 2.47).

9   In the **Category** section, check that **Number** is selected. In the **Decimal Places** section, enter the required number of decimal places or use the up/down arrows.

10  Click **OK**.

 **How to...** *format text on a chart (chart title, x- and y-axis titles, legend, text box)*

1   Click on the relevant text box in the chart to select it.

2   Square handles appear around the text box.

3   If you need to format only some of the text, highlight the relevant text within the text box.

4   In the Menu bar, click on **Format**.

If the selected text is in the title, the first item in the Format menu will display as **Selected Chart Title**. Similarly, if the selected text is in a text box, the first item will display as **Selected Object**.

5   In the drop-down menu, click **Selected Chart Title/Object**. A **Format Chart Title/Object** dialogue box displays.

6   Select the required formatting (Figure 2.48).

Note that some formatting options can be selected from the Formatting toolbar, e.g. bold, font size, font type.

7   Click **OK**.

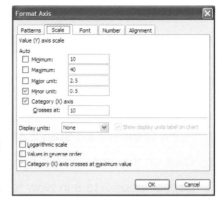

**FIGURE 2.46** Setting the intervals and values in the Format Axis dialogue box

**FIGURE 2.47** The Number tab in the Format Axis dialogue box

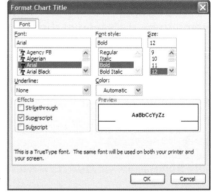

**FIGURE 2.48** Setting the text formatting in the Format Chart Title dialogue box

In the file **incidents**, apply the following formatting to your bar chart titled **CAUSE OF INCIDENT AS A PERCENTAGE OF TOTAL INCIDENTS IN THE 21ST CENTURY**.

1 Format the **y-axis** as follows:

- minimum value: **10**
- maximum value: **40**
- interval: **2.5**
- numbers set to **1 decimal place.**

2 Format the ST in **21ST** in the title to be **superscript**.

3 Save the updated chart.

---

**▶▶ How to...** *remove the fill from the plot area (optional)*

Excel usually displays the plot area as grey. To make the chart clearer and to save printer ink the fill can be removed.

1 Hover your mouse pointer anywhere in the grey plot area, a **Plot Area** Tool tip displays.

2 Double-click in the plot area.

3 A **Format Plot Area** dialogue box opens (Figure 2.49).

4 In the **Area** section, click **None**.

5 Click **OK**.

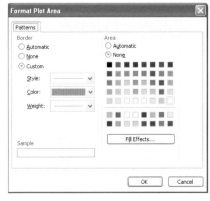

FIGURE 2.49 The Format Plot Area dialogue box

**TIP!**

You may select white instead of None.

---

In your file **incidents**, make the following changes to your bar chart titled **CAUSE OF INCIDENT AS A PERCENTAGE OF TOTAL INCIDENTS IN THE 21ST CENTURY**.

1 Remove the fill of the plot area.

2 Save the updated file keeping the same filename.

3 Set the chart option to Print in black and white (refer to How to... set the option to print in black and white on page 60 if you need to recap on these skills).

4 Print the chart.

5 Do not save the updated file.

**TIP!**

Fill effects are applied after the chart is created.

1   In your chart, click on one of the bars. A square dot displays in all the bars for that series.

2   Double-click on one of the selected bars.

3   A **Format Data Series** dialogue box opens (Figure 2.50).

4   In the dialogue box, click the **Patterns** tab.

5   Click the **Fill Effects** button.

6   A **Fill Effects** dialogue box will open (Figure 2.51).

7   In the dialogue box, click the **Pattern** tab.

8   Click on one of the patterns to select it.

9   The pattern sample will display.

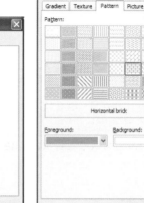

FIGURE 2.50 The Patterns tab in the Format Data Series dialogue box

FIGURE 2.51 The Fill Effects dialogue box

10   Click **OK** to close the **Fill Effects** dialogue box.

11   Click **OK** to close the **Format Data Series** dialogue box.

12   Repeat for the remaining sets of bars.

**TIP!**

In the Fill Effects dialogue box, click the drop-down arrow next to Foreground and/or Background to choose a different colour (Figure 2.51).

▶▶ **How to...** *set the text orientation on the x-axis*

1   Hover the mouse pointer over any of the x-axis labels.

2   A **Category Axis** Tool tip will display. Double-click on the label.

3   A **Format Axis** dialogue box displays.

4   Click on the **Alignment** tab (Figure 2.52).

5   Click in the **Degrees** box and enter the required number.

6   Check the preview.

7   Click **OK**.

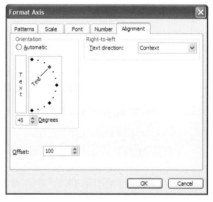

FIGURE 2.52 The Alignment tab in the Format Axis dialogue box

In your saved file **incidents**, make the following changes to your bar chart titled **CAUSE OF INCIDENT AS A PERCENTAGE OF TOTAL INCIDENTS IN THE 21ST CENTURY**.

1   Apply a different fill effect to each of the four series so that the legend and the bars will be clearly distinguishable when printed.

2   Set the orientation of the x-axis labels to **45˚**.

3   Save the updated chart keeping the same filename.

4   Print the chart.

5   Close the file.

Check your printout against the solution on the CD-ROM.

## ASSESS YOUR SKILLS – Create comparative charts

By working through Section 2 you will have learnt the skills listed below. Read each item to help you decide how confident you feel about each skill.

- ○ understand comparative charts
- ○ identify the parts of a comparative chart
- ○ understand the selection of data for comparative charts
- ○ use the Chart Wizard to create a comparative chart
- ○ enter the chart title, x-axis and y-axis titles
- ○ define the data series for a chart (remove unwanted series, select the data to be plotted on the x- and y- axis, select the name for legend items)
- ○ enter the chart title, x-axis and y-axis titles
- ○ format the axis values (scale, intervals, numbers)
- ○ format text
- ○ remove the fill from the plot area
- ○ use a pattern fill for the bars
- ○ set the text orientation.

If you think that you need more practice on any of the skills in the above list, go back and work through the skill(s) again.

If you feel confident, move on to Section 3.

**In this section you will learn how to:**

- *understand line-column graphs*
- *identify the parts of a line-column graph*
- *create a line-column graph*
- *enter the chart title, x-axis and y-axis titles*
- *display the legend*
- *select the chart location*
- *format the line(s)*
- *format the markers.*

## Line-column graphs

Line-column graphs are used to show a comparison of related data. One or more sets of data can be displayed as column(s) and another set as a line. Line-column graphs are usually used to show a comparison of data  displayed as bar(s) against a benchmark, displayed as a line.

### Parts of a line-column graph

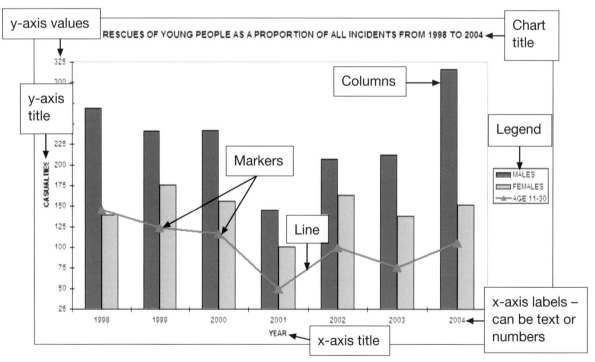

FIGURE 2.54 The parts of a line-column graph

FIGURE 2.54 Line - Column selected in the Custom Types tab of the Chart Wizard dialogue box

## How to... *create a line-column graph*

1 In the datafile, select only the relevant range of cells.
2 Click the **Chart Wizard** icon .
3 The Chart Wizard **Step 1 of 4** dialogue box will open.
4 Click the **Custom Types** tab, scroll down the list and select **Line-Column** (Figure 2.54).
5 Click **Next**.
6 The Chart Wizard **Step 2 of 4** dialogue box will open.
7 A preview of the chart displays, check that the preview is correct.

If the preview is incorrect, you *must* define the data series before continuing. Refer to How to... define the data series on pages 65–67 before proceeding to the Chart Wizard Step 3 of 4.

8 If the preview is correct, click **Next**.
9 The Chart Wizard **Step 3 of 4** dialogue box will display.
10 In the **Titles** tab, enter the Chart title, x-axis title and y-axis title.
11 Click the **Legend** tab, ensure there is a tick in the **Show Legend** box.
12 Click **Next**.
13 The Chart Wizard **Step 4 of 4** dialogue box will display.
14 Click the button for **As new sheet**.
15 Optional: name the chart.
16 Click **Finish**.

## Check your understanding *Create a line-column graph*

1 Open the file called **age** and save it as an Excel file using the filename **young**
2 Ensure that all data is displayed in full.
3 Create a **line-column graph** to plot the number of **MALES** and **FEMALES** (as columns) with the numbers of people **AGE 11–30** (as a line) from **1998** to **2004**

Check your data selection. The range selected should be **A3:H5** and **A10:H10**.

4 Title the chart: **RESCUES OF YOUNG PEOPLE AS A PROPORTION OF ALL INCIDENTS FROM 1998 TO 2004**
5 Title the x-axis: **YEAR**
6 Title the y-axis: **CASUALTIES**
7 Display a legend showing: **MALES    FEMALES    AGE 11–30**.
8 Format the **y-axis** as follows:

- minimum value: **25**
- interval: **25**
- maximum value: **325**
- numbers set to **0** decimal places.

9 Set the chart orientation to **landscape**.
10 Enter your **name** and an **automatic filename** as a footer.
11 Save the file keeping the filename **young**

# Formatting lines and markers on a line-column graph

It is important that the data will be clearly distinctive on the printout – especially if it is printed on a black and white printer. To make the data distinctive, the line and/or marker style can be changed.

**▶▶ How to...** *format a line on a line-column graph*

1 Hover your mouse pointer over the line on the graph.

2 Double-click on the line.

3 A **Format Data Series** dialogue box will open (Figure 2.55).

4 Click the **Patterns** tab.

5 In the **Line** section, click the **Custom** button.

6 Click the drop-down arrow next to **Style**. Choose a line style.

7 Click the drop-down arrow next to **Weight**. Choose a thick line.

8 Optional: click the drop-down arrow next to **Color** to change the line colour.

9 To format the markers see below, or click **OK**.

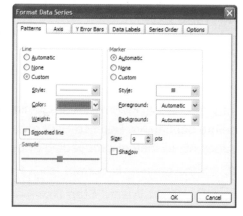

**FIGURE 2.55** The Patterns tab in the Format Data Series dialogue box

**▶▶ How to...** *format the markers on a line-column graph*

1 Hover your mouse pointer over the line on the graph.

2 Double-click on the line to display a menu.

3 In the **Format Data Series** dialogue box, in the **Marker** section, click the **Custom** button.

4 Click the drop-down arrow next to **Style**. Choose one of the marker styles.

5 To change the marker colour, click the drop-down arrow next to **Foreground** and/or **Background**.

6 To change the marker size, click in the **Size** box and enter the required size or use the up/down arrows.

7 Click **OK**.

**TIP!**

If Format Data Point displays instead of Format Data Series, you have clicked on a marker. Click Cancel. Left-click in the plot area to deselect the marker, then hover the mouse pointer over the line and double-click to display the correct dialogue box.

In your saved file **young**, format your chart titled **RESCUES OF YOUNG PEOPLE AS A PROPORTION OF ALL INCIDENTS FROM 1998 TO 2004** as follows.

1   Format the line so it appears as a solid, dark line with thick line weighting.

2   Format the markers as large triangles (e.g. size 12) in a dark shade. The line and markers must be clearly visible across the bars.

3   Make sure that the legend clearly identifies the three data sets.

4   Save the files keeping the same filename.

5   Close the file.

6   Check your printout against the solution on the CD-ROM.

## ASSESS YOUR SKILLS – Create line-column graphs

By working through Section 3 you will have learnt the skills listed below. Read each item to help you decide how confident you feel about each skill.

○ understand line-column graphs

○ identify the parts of a line-column graph

○ create a line-column graph

○ enter the chart title, x-axis and y-axis titles

○ display the legend

○ select the chart location

○ format the line(s)

○ format the markers.

If you feel that you need more practice on any of the skills in the above list, go back and work through the skill(s) again.

If you feel confident, move on to Section 4.

**In this section you will learn how to:**

- understand xy scatter graphs
- identify the parts of an xy scatter graph
- understand the selection of data for xy scatter graphs
- use the Chart Wizard to create an xy scatter graph
- enter the chart title, x-axis and y-axis titles
- join the data points on an xy scatter graph
- add a text box to a graph.

## xy scatter graphs

xy scatter graphs are used to plot **pairs** of co-ordinates. On an xy scatter graph, a point (shown by a marker) is plotted where the x value meets the y value. xy scatter graphs are usually plotted using two sets of numeric data (i.e. numeric data is displayed on the y-axis and the x-axis). On other charts (e.g. line graphs, etc.), the data on the x-axis is usually descriptive (i.e. text).

xy scatter graphs can be used for two purposes:

- to plot a definite relationship between two *variables* (e.g. the cost of chocolate in relation to sales)
- to determine if there is any relationship between the two variables.

**What does it mean?**

**Co-ordinate:** a co-ordinate is made up of an x value and a y value.

**Variable:** an item that can have many different values (e.g. each person has a different height and weight).

## Parts of an xy scatter graph

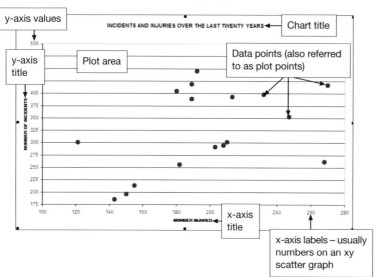

**FIGURE 2.56** Parts of an xy scatter graph

1 In the datafile, select only the relevant range of cells.

2 Click the **Chart Wizard** icon 📊.

3 The Chart Wizard **Step 1 of 4** dialogue box will open.

4 In the **Standard Types** tab, in the Chart type section, click on **XY (Scatter)** (Figure 2.57).

5 In the Chart sub-type section, check that **Scatter** is selected.

6 Click **Next**.

7 The Chart Wizard **Step 2 of 4** dialogue box will open.

8 A preview of the chart displays, check the preview.

If the preview is incorrect, you **must** define the data series before continuing. Refer to How to... define the data series on pages 65–67 before proceeding to the Chart Wizard Step 3 of 4.

9 If the preview is correct, click **Next**.

10 The Chart Wizard **Step 3 of 4** dialogue box will open.

11 Click the **Titles** tab.

12 In the **Chart Title** box, enter the title.

13 In the **Category (X) axis** box, enter the x-axis title.

14 In the **Value (Y) axis** box, enter the y-axis title.

15 Click the **Legend** tab.

16 Click to place or remove the tick in the **Show legend** box as required for the chart.

17 Click **Next**.

18 The Chart Wizard **Step 4 of 4** dialogue box will open.

19 Click the button for **As new sheet**.

20 Optional: enter a name for the sheet.

21 Click **Finish**.

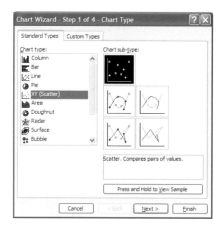

FIGURE 2.57 XY (Scatter) in the Chart Wizard dialogue box

**TIP!**

Look at the figures in the original datafile to make sure the data points plotted on the chart have been plotted correctly.

1   Open the file called **rescues**.

2   Save the file as an Excel file using the filename **20years**

3   Select the data to create a chart to show the number of **INCIDENTS** against the numbers **INJURED** from **1985 to 2004**.

Check your selection of data. You should have selected the following range of cells: **From C2 to V3**

4   Create an **xy scatter graph**.

5   Title the chart: **INCIDENTS AND INJURIES OVER THE LAST TWENTY YEARS**

6   Title the x-axis: **NUMBER INJURED**

7   Title the y-axis: **NUMBER OF INCIDENTS**

8   Do not display a legend.

9   Create the chart on a sheet that is separate from the data source.

10  Set the chart orientation to **landscape**.

11  Format the **x-axis** as follows:

   ○ minimum value: **100**
   ○ maximum value: **280**
   ○ interval: **20**

   numbers set to **0** decimal places.

12  Format the **y-axis** as follows:

   ○ minimum value: **175**
   ○ maximum value: **550**
   ○ interval: **25**

   numbers set to **0 decimal places**.

13  Ensure that the markers on the graph are clearly visible as **circles**.

14  Optional: remove the fill of the plot area.

15  In the footer enter **your name**, **your centre number**, an **automatic date** and an **automatic filename**.

16  Save the chart.

17  Print the chart.

Check your printout against the solution on the CD-ROM.

 **How to...** *join the data points on an xy scatter graph*

1 Hover the mouse pointer over one of the data points and double-click.

2 **Format Data Series** dialogue box displays.

3 Select the **Patterns** tab (Figure 2.58).

4 In the **Line** section, click the **Custom** button.

5 Click the drop-down arrow next to **Style** box and select the required line style.

6 Click the drop-down arrow next to **Weight** and select the required thickness of the line.

7 If you need to remove the markers, see below, otherwise click **OK**.

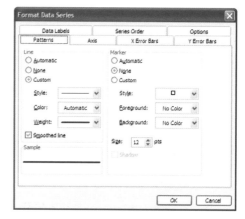

FIGURE 2.58 The Patterns tab in the Format Data Series dialogue box

 **How to...** *remove the markers*

1 In the **Format Data Series** dialogue box, in the **Marker** section, click **None**.

2 Click **OK**.

 **How to...** *add a text box to a graph*

1 Ensure that the **Drawing toolbar** is displayed.

2 From the Drawing toolbar, select the **Text Box** icon ⌐ (Figure 2.59).

FIGURE 2.59 The Drawing toolbar

3 Move the mouse pointer into the plot area and draw a frame for the text box. Ensure that the text box is not drawn in a position where it will touch or overlap any existing lines on the graph.

4 A cursor will display in the text box, enter the required text.

5 To change the size of the text box, click and drag one of the round handles on the side of the text box.

6 To move the text box, click and drag the frame of the text box.

**TIP!**

Select a thick line weighting.

**TIP!**

To display the Drawing toolbar click **View** in the Menu bar, select **Toolbars** from the drop-down menu and select **Drawing**.

**TIP!**

Displaying a border around a text box is optional. To remove a border, select the text box, click the drop-down arrow next the Line Color icon on the Drawing toolbar 🖌 and select **No Line**. To select a line colour for the border, click on a colour square.

1 Open your saved file named **incidents**. You are going to create a second chart in this file.

2 Select the worksheet named **cause**. (Click on the tab named **cause** at the bottom left of the screen.)

3 Select the data to create a chart to show the **CHANGE FROM PREVIOUS YEAR** against the YEARS from **1998–2004**.

Check your selection of data. You should have selected the cells shown in Figure 2.60.

4 Create an **xy scatter graph**.

5 Title the chart: **CHANGE IN THE NUMBER OF INJURIES FROM PREVIOUS YEAR**

6 Title the x-axis: **YEAR**

7 Title the y-axis: **CHANGE**

| | | INJURED | CHANGE FROM PREVIOUS YEAR |
|---|---|---|---|
| 14 | 1997 | 245 | 0 |
| 15 | 1998 | 207 | -38 |
| 16 | 1999 | 176 | -31 |
| 17 | 2000 | 193 | 17 |
| 18 | 2001 | 124 | -69 |
| 19 | 2002 | 180 | 56 |
| 20 | 2003 | 189 | 9 |
| 21 | 2004 | 211 | 22 |

FIGURE 2.60 Selected cells in the cause worksheet

8 Do not display a legend.

9 Create the chart on a sheet that is separate from the data source.

10 Set the chart orientation to **portrait**.

11 Join the points on the scatter graph together to produce a solid line with no markers.

12 Format the **x-axis** as follows:
- minimum value: **1998**
- maximum value: **2004**

13 Format the **y-axis** as follows:
- minimum value: **-75**
- maximum value: **75**
- interval: **10**

numbers set to **0 decimal places**.

14 In the plot area, insert a text box with the words: **EFFECT OF FOOT AND MOUTH DISEASE**

Ensure that the text box does not overlap/touch the line.

15 Optional: remove the fill of the plot area.

16 Insert **your name** as a header or footer.

17 Save the chart.

18 Print the chart.

Check your printout against the solution on the CD-ROM.

**TIP!** Selecting the option for **Smoothed line** is optional.

# ASSESS YOUR SKILLS – Create xy scatter graphs

By working through Section 4 you will have learnt the skills listed below. Read each item to help you decide how confident you feel about each skill.

- ○ understand xy scatter graphs
- ○ identify the parts of an xy scatter graph
- ○ understand the selection of data for xy scatter graphs
- ○ use the Chart Wizard to create an xy scatter graph
- ○ enter the chart title, x-axis and y-axis titles
- ○ join the data points on an xy scatter graph
- ○ add a text box to a graph.

If you think that you need more practice on any of the skills in the above list, go back and work through the skill(s) again.

If you feel confident, do the Build-up tasks on pages 82–85 and Practice task on the CD-ROM.

The files for the Build-up tasks can be found in a folder named **U2datafiles_buildtasks**. You will need the file **gcse_stat** to complete this task.

You have been asked to produce a report on GCSE statistics for a number of schools in the southern region.

Unless otherwise instructed you may use any readable font, alignment, emphasis and size to suit the data.

**1** Open the file **gcse_stat** and save it in as an Excel file using the filename **stats1**

**2 a** Use text wrap to display the column labels below on **2 lines** – do not split words.

**School Measure
Compared to Benchmark**

**b** Ensure that all data is displayed in full.

**c** Format the data items listed as follows:

| LABEL | SIZE | COLUMNS |
|---|---|---|
| GCSE Achievement Statistics 2005 | Large | Centred across all columns containing data Columns A–I Framed by a border |
| Value Added | Medium | A–B |
| Schools in South County | Medium | A–I Framed by a border |

**3** In the **Schools in South County** section, in the **Total column**, use a function to calculate the **Total** of the three **subjects**: English, Mathematics and Science for each of the schools.

**4 a** In the **Schools in South County** section, in the **Average column**, use a function to calculate the **Average** of the three **subjects** for the first school.

**b** Replicate this formula for all the other schools.

**5** In the **Value Added** section, name the cell containing the figure for GCSE as **value_added**

**6** Save the spreadsheet keeping the filename **stats1**

1 You will need the following files for this task:

  ○ the file called **stats1** that you saved in Build-up task 1 (alternatively, you may use the file **stats1** provided in the worked copies folder)

  ○ the file **benchmark**.

2 a Open the file **benchmark** and save it in as an Excel file using the filename **nat_stats**

  b Save using the new filename **stats2** the file **stats1**

3 In the **stats2** spreadsheet, a value added figure is to be taken into consideration for schools in the southern region due to the location of the schools.

  a In the **Schools in South County** section, in the **School Measure** column, use a formula to calculate the figure to be used to indicate a school's performance. This figure is calculated as follows:

  Add the average figure to the named cell **value_added**, then multiply the result by 105%.

  b Replicate this formula for all the other schools.

4 The report needs to show how a school's results compare with the national benchmark. To calculate this figure you will need to link the two spreadsheets and use an absolute cell reference.

  a In the **Schools in South County** section, in the **Compared to Benchmark** column, use a function to calculate whether a school's measurable value is higher or lower than the national benchmark.

  This figure is calculated as follows:

  IF the **School Measure** figure in the **stats2** spreadsheet is greater than the figure for the **GCSE Average** in the **nat_stats** spreadsheet, return the value **higher**, if it is not, return the value **lower**.

  b Replicate this formula for the other schools.

5 a Format the figures in the **Total, Average** and **School Measure** columns as **integer** (zero decimal places) with no currency symbol.

  b Format the column label and all the data in the **Compared to Benchmark** column to be centred horizontally.

6 a Insert your **name**, **centre number**, and an **automatic filename** as a header or footer.

  b Set the page orientation to **landscape.**

  c Save your spreadsheet keeping the filename **stats2**

  d Ensure all data is displayed in full. Print a copy of the spreadsheet **stats2** showing all the figures.

7 You have been asked for a printout of the formulae of your spreadsheet **stats2**.

  a In the **Schools in the South County** section, hide all the information in the columns from **Type** to **Science** (columns B to E).

    b  In the **Value Added** section hide all the information in the rows from **Value Added** to **A2** (rows 3 to 6).

    c  Display the formulae.

    d  Check that the page orientation is **landscape**.

    e  Display **gridlines** and **row and column headings**.

    f  Ensure that all formulae are fully displayed **on one page** and clearly legible.

    g  Save the file with the filename **statsform**.

    h  Print the formulae on one page.

8  Close any open files.

---

## BUILD-UP TASK ③ *Filter and sort data*

You will need the file **stats2** that you saved in Build-up task 2 to complete this task. (Alternatively, you may use the file **stats2** provided in the worked copies folder.)

You have been asked to present data about comprehensive schools only.

1  Open the file **stats2** and save it using the filename **comps**

2  Filter the data in the **Type** column to find all **Comprehensive** schools only.

3  Sort the data in the **School Measure** column in **descending** order ensuring that the corresponding data is sorted correctly.

4  In the **Value Added** section, delete the entire rows for **AS** and **A2**.

5  a  Ensure all data is displayed in full.

    b  Display **gridlines** and **row and column headings**.

    c  Insert your **name, centre number** and an **automatic filename** as a footer.

6  a  Save your spreadsheet keeping the filename **comps**

    b  Print a copy of the filtered spreadsheet in **landscape** orientation showing all the filtered data in full.

7  Close any open files.

---

## BUILD-UP TASK ④ *Create an exploded pie chart*

You will need the file **tests** to complete this task.

You have been asked by the Head of Faculty to produce an exploded pie chart showing the class average mark for tests done by students for the whole academic year.

1  a  Open the datafile **tests** and save it in as an Excel file using the filename **marks**

    b  Display all data in full.

2  Using the **CLASS AVERAGE** for the **five tests** from **INITIAL ASSESSMENT** to **END OF YEAR** create an exploded **pie chart**.

a  Title the chart: **CLASS AVERAGE MARK FOR TESTS FOR ACADEMIC YEAR FOR THE LAST 10 YEARS**.

b  Each sector must be clearly labelled with a data label and the **actual value**.

c  Do not display a legend.

d  Create the chart on a sheet that is separate from the data source.

e  Pull out the smallest sector of the pie chart so that it is further away from the rest of the chart.

3  In the plot area, insert a text box with the words:

**LOWEST MARK TERM 3**

Ensure the text box does not overlap/touch any labels, values or sectors.

4  a  Insert your **name, centre number** and an **automatic filename** as a header or footer.

b  Save the file.

c  Print one copy of the chart.

5  Close the file.

 **BUILD-UP TASK 5** *Create a line-column graph*

The Head of Faculty has asked you to analyse some data on student test marks at the beginning and the end of the academic year.

1  Open your saved file called **marks**.

2  Create a **line-column graph** to plot the data for the **INITIAL ASSESSMENT** and the **END OF YEAR** test as **columns** against the data for the **CANDIDATE AVERAGE** from **2000 to 2005** inclusive.

a  Title the graph: **COMPARISON OF RESULTS AT BEGINNING AND END OF YEAR**

b  Label the x-axis: **YEAR**

c  Label the y-axis: **MARK**

d  Create the graph on a sheet that is separate from the data source.

3  Format the line as a thick, dark, solid line with markers.

4  Format the y-axis as follows:

minimum value:   **50**
maximum value:   **100**
interval:        **10**

5  Insert your **name, centre number** and **filename** as a header or footer.

6  Save the file keeping the filename **marks**

7  Print one copy of the line-column graph.

Now work through the Practice task on the CD-ROM.

## Definition of terms

**Absolute cell reference** A cell address that does not change in relation to the position of the formula in the spreadsheet. Both the row number and column letter are preceded by a $ sign (e.g. $A$1).

**Active cell** A single cell that is currently selected, displays with a darker border.

**Active window** The window in which the current task is being performed.

**Adjacent** Cells which are next to each other.

**Alignment** The position of data within a cell.

**Amend** To make changes to data.

**Automatic fields** A code that can be inserted, by the click of an icon, that instructs Excel to insert items in the document automatically, for example the date, filename, page numbers.

**AutoSum** An automatic function that calculates the total value of a range of adjacent cells.

**AVERAGE** A function that calculates the mean (medium) value of a range of cells.

**Bar chart** A chart that displays data as vertical bars to show data changes over a period of time, comparisons between individual items or comparisons between data.

**Brackets** Used in a formula to force Excel to perform calculations in a particular order. A range of cells in a function is enclosed in brackets.

**Category axis** x-axis of a chart (usually the horizontal axis).

**Category labels** Labels displayed on the x-axis that describe the data.

**Cell** A spreadsheet consists of rows and columns, a cell is formed where they cross. Data is entered into a cell.

**Cell reference (Cell address)** The address of a cell, consisting of the column letter followed by the row number. A cell reference identifies the location of values to be used in a calculation.

**Chart** A pictorial representation of numerical data.

**Chart heading** Chart title.

**Chart location** Where a graph is displayed, it can be on the worksheet (spreadsheet) or as a separate sheet.

**Chart title** The chart heading, provides information about the chart content.

**Chart Wizard** An automated feature for producing charts easily. It guides the user through a series of windows to create a chart.

**Clear contents** Deleting the contents of the cells. If entire rows/columns are cleared, the row/column remains but all cells in the row/column are empty (blank).

**Column** A line of cells running vertically down a spreadsheet, identified by letters.

**Column chart** Excel's name for a vertical bar chart.

**Column headings** The letters used to identify columns.

**Column labels** The titles that identify the data in a column.

**Contiguous data** Cells that are next to each other. When a block of cells can be selected for the creation of a chart, this is referred to as contiguous data.

**Co-ordinate** Applies to the data used for xy scatter graphs: a co-ordinate is made up of an x value and a y value.

**COUNT** A function that counts the number of cells containing numeric data.

**COUNTA** A function that counts the number of cells that contain data (numeric or alphabetic).

**COUNTIF** A function that counts the number of cells that meet a specified condition.

**Criterion** A selection condition used to find specific data.

**.csv** Comma separated value or comma separated variable. Tabular data saved in a format that can be read by a number of applications. A comma usually separates the data in each column. Only the data (text and numbers) is preserved, formatting will be lost.

**Currency format** Numbers are displayed with a monetary symbol in front of them to show the currency used in a country (e.g. £).

**Customised** Changes made to the 'default' settings to suit the individual user.

**Datafile** File that contains data (which can be in any format). In this unit a datafile is provided for use when creating spreadsheets and graphs.

**Data label** The name (description) of each data point.

**Data series** A set of related data points to be plotted on a chart.

**Decimal places** The number of figures displayed after the decimal point.

**Default** The setting that a computer program (or system) will use unless it is changed or 'customised'.

**Delete row/column** Removing the cells completely, the remaining row numbers or column letters are automatically re-numbered/re-labelled.

**Drag** The action of clicking and holding a selected item and sliding it to a new position by moving the mouse.

**Fill handle** A square on the bottom right corner of a cell that enables copying of the cell contents or formula to adjacent cells.

**Find** A method of searching for specified data.

**Find and Replace** A method of searching for specified data and replacing it with a specified alternative everywhere it appears.

**Folder** An area created to store and organise files.

**Format** The display on a spreadsheet (e.g. column labels, numbers, etc.) or on a chart (e.g. data points, lines, text labels, etc.).

**Formatting** Changing the layout and appearance of text and/or numbers and/or cells.

**Formula** A calculation in a spreadsheet, can use values and/or cell references.

**Formula bar** A bar above the main worksheet area that displays the actual content of the active cell.

**Formulae** More than one formula. Sometimes referred to as formulas.

**Function** A pre-defined formula that carries out a specific calculation, for example SUM, COUNT, AVERAGE.

**Generic file type (Generic file format)** A file saved in a format that can be read by most computer systems and in a large number of software applications.

**Headers and footers** The area in the top and bottom margin of the page. Items placed in headers and footers will appear at the top and bottom of every page. See also automatic fields.

**Hover** To position the mouse over an object/area on the screen.

**IF** A function that returns one value if a condition is met and another value if the condition is not met.

**Insert row/column** A new row or column is inserted between existing data in a spreadsheet. Row numbers or column letters are automatically re-numbered/re-labelled when the new row/column is inserted.

**Integer** A whole number i.e. no (zero) decimal places.

**Interval** The gap between numbers on a value axis.

**Label** In a spreadsheet: the row or column titles. In a graph: text entries that describe the contents of areas of the chart (e.g. title, legend, etc.).

**Legend** A key, it is a text box in the chart area that identifies the patterns or colours for each data series in a chart.

**Line graph** A graph that displays data series as a line.

**Maintaining integrity of data** Ensuring that all data that belongs together, stays together when data is manipulated or a sort is performed.

**Major unit** Excel's term for interval.

**Markers** The data points on a line graph.

**Marquee** A flashing dashed border around selected cell(s).

**Mathematical operator** One of four mathematical symbols: * / + - (multiply, divide, add, subtract).

**MAX** A function that returns the largest number from a range of cells.

**Menu** A list of items.

**MIN** A function that returns the smallest number from a range of cells.

**Mixed cell reference** A cell reference where one of the components is relative and the other is absolute. For example: $A1 – the reference will always be made to the column (A) but the row reference will change in relation to the position of the formula in the spreadsheet.

**Name box** Appears on the left of the formula bar, displays the cell address or the name given to a cell.

**Named cell** A cell that has been given a name.

**Named cell reference** A reference to a named cell. The values in the named cell will always be used in calculations regardless of the position the named cell occupies in the spreadsheet.

**Named range** A range of cells that has been given a name.

**Native file type (native file format)** The default format that datafiles will be saved in, unless an alternative format is selected. For example, the native file format for a file saved in Microsoft Excel would be .xls.

**Negative number** A number below zero, usually preceded with a minus sign.

**Non-contiguous data** Non-adjacent data.

**Non-generic file type** Also referred to as 'native' or 'normal' file type. The file type in which the file will be saved by 'default' (unless you change it!).

**Normal file type** The file type in which documents will be saved, unless the user specifies an alternative format. The 'normal' file type for an Excel file is .xls.

**Orientation** The way paper is displayed, can be portrait (shortest side at the top) or landscape (widest side at the top).

**Print Preview** Displays on screen how a spreadsheet or graph/chart will look like when printed.

**Range** A group (series) of cells. In a spreadsheet formula a range of adjacent cells is enclosed in brackets with a colon in between the first and last cell in the range (e.g. (F3:H3)).

**Relative cell reference** A cell reference that changes in relation to the position of the formula in the spreadsheet. When a formula is copied over cell(s), the formulas change automatically. The calculation is performed on cells relative (next to) the copied formula.

**Replicate** To copy.

**Row** A line of cells running horizontally across a spreadsheet, identified by numbers.

**Row headings** The grey row numbers.

**Scale** The minimum and maximum values (numbers) displayed on an axis.

**Sector** A slice on a pie chart.

**Sort** Re-ordering of data in ascending or descending order. When sorting, ensure that all associated data is also sorted, this is referred to as maintaining the integrity of data.

**Spellcheck** A tool in Excel that automatically checks words against a large dictionary.

**Spreadsheet** Is used to manipulate figures, a spreadsheet program processes tabular information, usually numbers. All tasks involving the use of numbers can be done on a spreadsheet.

**Subfolder** A folder within a folder.

**Submenu** A further list of choices available from some menu items.

**Subscript** Text that appears smaller and in a lower position than the rest of the text on a line.

**SUM** A function that adds all the values in a range of cells.

**SUMIF** A function that adds all the values of cells that meet a specified condition.

**Superscript** Text that appears smaller and in a higher position than the rest of the text on a line.

**Tab (in a window)** A marker (like a file marker) to indicate that more options are available by clicking on the tab. A window may have a number of tabs, these are the different sections of the window. To view the options in that section, click on the tab name.

**Taskbar** A bar usually at the bottom of the screen, running the length of the Desktop, it shows which tasks the computer is performing.

**Text orientation** The angle of the data labels.

**Title bar** Is displayed at the top of a program window, it shows the program icon, name and filename.

**Tool tip** When the mouse hovers over an item the program displays a tip, usually with a yellow background, showing the name of an object on the screen.

**Truncate** Data not displayed in full.

**User area** The workspace on a computer for the storage of files. Examples are: the My Documents folder, a network drive, a floppy disk or hard disk drive.

**Value** A number entered into a cell or a result of a calculation.

**Value axis** The y-axis on a chart (usually the vertical axis).

**Values (chart values)** Numbers displayed next to pie chart sectors or on the y-axis of a bar chart or line graph.

**Workbook** A file that contains one or more worksheets (spreadsheets). A workbook allows all related spreadsheets and graphs to be stored in one file.

**Worksheet** Excel term for a spreadsheet. The main sheet that is used in Excel to store and work with data. A worksheet consists of cells that are organised into columns and rows. In Excel a worksheet is always stored in a workbook.

**x-axis** The horizontal axis on a bar chart or line graph.

**x-axis title** The name displayed on the category axis.

**y-axis** The value axis on a chart (value axis).

**y-axis title** The name displayed on the value axis.

# Index